Creeds in
Collision

Creeds in
Collision

R. Benjamin Garrison

Nashville   *Abingdon Press*   *New York*

CREEDS IN COLLISION

Copyright © 1967 by Abingdon Press

Library of Congress Catalog Card Number: 67-14982

Scripture quotations unless otherwise noted are
from the Revised Standard Version of the Bible,
copyrighted 1946 and 1952 by the Division of
Christian Education, National Council of Churches,
and are used by permission.

SET UP, PRINTED, AND BOUND BY THE
PARTHENON PRESS, AT NASHVILLE,
TENNESSEE, UNITED STATES OF AMERICA

To
my grandfather
Ben Kendall
who gave me a name
and a Name

Preface

In our time many of the creeds which contend for the allegiance of men are not the belief systems of one organized religion or another. Indeed a case can be made for the contention that the sternest bids for intellectual attention are being proffered by men and modes of belief themselves quite self-consciously *not* religious in any usual sense of the word.

They are no less creeds for all that. Like the traditional creeds they claim to speak from experience. (For instance, "despair" in the existentialist's lexicon is not so much an idea to be explained as it is a pain to be explored.) Like

7

the religious belief systems, they endeavor to express this prior experience in terms which others can understand, pursue, and perhaps adopt. And, like all creeds, they seek to elicit from men a conjoining response, although not necessarily a "religious" one.

Furthermore and more importantly, they are live options. This little volume's title, *Creeds in Collision*, indicates the seriousness with which the author has endeavored to take the challenges and claims of the creeds under consideration. The word "collision" is quite deliberately chosen. Theodore M. Bernstein in his valuable and superb book, *The Careful Writer*, points out: "When two things *collide* they strike or dash against one another, i.e., both are in motion. A parked car cannot be one of the objects in a collision." [1]

In the same way secularism is a *moving* force in our world; humanism is mobile; Marxism is on the march; the radical right is active; existentialism is a nearly frenetic philosophy; playboyism, whatever form it may take, shivers with passion.

All of these can, I suppose, be deplored. They cannot be ignored. What I have tried to do herein is to state the particular credal position as fairly as possible and to indicate where and how it runs contrary to—that is, collides with—the Christian faith as I understand it. Others

[1] (New York: Atheneum Publishers, 1965), p. 109.

have written more profoundly than I on any or all of these idea systems. Whatever merit the present effort possesses lies in the degree to which it expresses these creeds and this critique in nontechnical language for the general reader.

No one writes a book like this without help. Mine has been substantial, and I am glad to say so: Professors Gardiner and Ruth Stillwell and Mrs. Raymond Knell read nearly all of what follows with eyes open and red pencil ready for stylistic infelicities. My colleague in campus ministry, the Rev. Richard Feldman, examined the chapters on secularism and existentialism and offered his customary trenchant and helpful (if not always comforting) comments. Professor Norman A. Graebner, distinguished diplomatic historian of the University of Illinois, perused and improved the chapter on Marxism. Anson Mount of *Playboy* magazine discovered some factual errors in an earlier draft of chapter six and assisted even more with other matters of judgment.

Further, the congregation of the Wesley Methodist Church in Urbana-Champaign, Illinois, has forced me into the thoroughly pleasant habit of taking two weeks annually as study leave, thus making possible an extra margin of time and detachment for reading and writing. My faithful secretary, Mrs. Donald Alberts, has reduced my often indecipherable hieroglyphics to some measure of stenographic order. Finally there is—not at all "of course"

—my wife, who keeps the phonograph turned down and our children approximately quiet so that I can hear the bullfrogs and listen to the Muse.

It remains only to add the hope that this volume will also collide with the reader, clarifyingly.

R. BENJAMIN GARRISON
Chateau Chevaux
Springstead, Wisconsin
July, 1966

Contents

SECULARISM—GOD EMERITUS

The event was a retirement party for a professor. It was one of those sad-glad occasions at which in business or industry the honored guest is presented with a gold watch. In university circles they merely summarize his bibliography, reminding him that his longed-for days of leisure are about to begin. The guest of honor in the case I have in mind wondered aloud about the meaning of the stately term "professor emeritus." In answer he suggested in semi-whimsy that it is a state of "statutory senility."

To attend such a retirement celebration is to find around

you and in you a variety of contradictory thoughts and
feelings. You are grateful that the accomplishments of
the professor are being given public recognition; you
welcome the opportunity of seeing them standing side
by side all at once for everyone to observe and admire.
Nevertheless, you are regretful that this climax ceremonial-
ly marks a conclusion practically. The old man may go on
writing lectures, some of them quite as good as those he
wrote in his prime, but not many of them will be heard. He
may carry forward his research, but in all likelihood its influence will be limited and its prestige discounted by this
new word now a part of his title: professor *emeritus*. Some
residual authority will cling to him for a time, but his
days are numbered. He is an academic has-been. Here-
after he will be ignored.

This is the mood and tone I intend to suggest by the
title of this chapter: "Secularism—God Emeritus." Where
it prevails religion has been retired. We may gather in
order festively to celebrate—or at least nostalgically to
remember—God's doings in the past. (Easter and Christmas
need not be outlawed after all.) Nevertheless the time
has come to recognize that senility is upon the old God.
He is harmless enough and may therefore be permitted
to putter around a bit in what we formerly considered his
laboratory, the world. We do not, however, expect anything very vital, startling, or important from him in the
future.

We may even be melancholy about this. Whether God

is dead, as Sartre (echoing Nietzsche) would have it, or simply retired, as we prefer to suppose, in either case we wish he were not. Still we have neither the respite nor the resolution for sustained regret. Life must continue even without a living God. We shall not waste our energies in debate about the weight of his past contributions. We simply do not expect much from him in the future. We shall not oppose him, but we shall ignore him, as—it seems—we must. He is emeritus, retired, a spiritual has-been.

This is the temper and stance of secularism as I hear it, see it, feel it in my bones. It is a creed (often a positively ethical one, seldom a consciously religious one), a body of belief which collides with Christian faith. I propose therefore to examine it in this chapter.

It is probably wise to provide here an introductory parenthesis on what is becoming better known as the "new secularity." Its proponents are many, increasing, and considerable. In many respects I number myself among them. They hold that the Christian faith has made entirely too much, and entirely too little that is defensible, of the distinction between sacred and secular. "The world" is not an enemy but an opportunity. Christians are meant and sent to live out their lives in the world, which is to say, in the structures and categories of the secular. To suggest an analogy: Christians are to be in the world as galvanized nails in a building, holding it together but not corroded by its acids.

A distinction must be drawn between secularization and secularism. Secularization "is basically a liberating development"[1] freeing us to work and witness in terms of the street corner realities and the occupational facts of the everyday. It means we *do* take the world seriously and *are* willing to be in it as its galvanized nails. On the other hand, secularism sounds similar but is opposite. Instead of freeing us, it enslaves us. Instead of calling us to serve the world, it requires us to worship it.[2] It is so close-minded and dogmatic that it makes the average

[1] Harvey Cox, *The Secular City* (New York: The Macmillan Company, 1965), p. 20. Cox helpfully develops this distinction between secularization and secularism, dealing with the implications of both, particularly of the former. Cox's volume is neither as revolutionary and monumental as some of its reviews claimed, nor as dangerous and negative as some of its detractors fear. In any case it is a needed volume (no small tribute) and will be around, to our embarrassment and profit, for some time.

Additionally the European theologian Arend Theodoor van Leeuwen writes, "It is helpful to make a clear distinction between secularization and secularism. The first is a continuing historical process, the second a fixed and absolutized ideology with a tendency toward pagan or nihilistic totalitarianism." *Christianity in World History* (New York: Charles Scribner's Sons, 1965), p. 334.

Cf. also Samuel H. Miller, *The Dilemma of Modern Belief* (New York: Harper & Row, 1963), especially Chapter I, "The Double Meaning of Secularity." The literature here is growing, in every way, rapidly.

[2] James Sellers comments in *Theological Ethics* (New York: The Macmillan Company, 1966), p. 148: "There is a good secularity and a bad secularism. It is healthy for men to know themselves as finite, living in time, and to be aware of the promise and peril of their own time. It is unhealthy (and unwhole) for men to be obsessed with their own age, forgetting the qualifications put upon us both by the past and future: this is a shallow sense of time, corresponding in the temporal dimension to the spatial attitude called provincialism."

religious dogmatism by contrast look like a multiple choice
question with several possible answers. Like most *isms*
it is a creed, and a rival creed at that, thus colliding with
the Christian faith. Hence its relevance to this study.

I

Secularism, to which we now turn more directly, comes
from a Latin word *saecula,* meaning an age or period in
history. Thus by descent secularism has come to mean the
habit of yielding to the spirit of the times. Putting it
that specifically is a little misleading, however, for secularism is not all that definite. It is an atmosphere more than
it is an object; like smog, it can be in the air for a long
time, poisoning our systems without our knowing it. One
recent writer has observed:

Indeed, it is possible that "secularism" itself, especially its negative aspects, is much more an unconscious than a conscious
process. It is possible that the unquestioned assumptions lying
behind the architecture, the town-planning, the industrial organization and its economic priorities, the educational pyramid,
the notions of social status, the grading of types of employment
and their relative attractiveness, the images of advertisement,
and the mythology of the hero (or the "anti-hero") in film, TV,
novel and drama—it is possible that the assumptions behind
these are the really determinative forces.[3]

[3]Martin Jarrett-Kerr, *The Secular Promise* (Philadelphia: Fortress
Press, 1965), p. 27.

It is more an attitude than it is an article of faith; like a resentment or a longing of which we are only half aware, it is difficult to pull out or pin down.

For a short period in England secularism existed as a separate, identifiable system of thought, clearly labeled as secularism. It was one of the reactions against the serious social wrongs of the period and against the churches' lack of sympathy with persons who suffered those wrongs. The term was coined by George Jacob Holyoake (1817-1906), who himself never seemed to share the dogmatic atheism of his day but was disgusted with fruitless religion.[4]

[4] It is still difficult to improve upon the brief statement of this philosophical phenomenon to be found in the *Encyclopedia of Religion and Ethics*, ed. James Hastings (13 vols.; New York: Charles Scribner's Sons, 1951), XI, 347 ff., "Secularism." It is revealing to note that Holyoake settled on the term "secularism" after considering but rejecting the term "limitationism." Leroy E. Lemker in *The Christian Faith and Secularism*, ed. J. Richard Spann (Nashville: Abingdon-Cokesbury Press, 1948) has also written, "The theoretical supports are to be found in that uneasy mixture of empiricism and naturalism characteristic of so much nineteenth-century thinking, to which the utilitarian and positivistic interpretations of religion, and the romantic conception of human nature, have imparted the quasi-religious accents of humanism. The secular arguments are an eclectic compound of subjectivism, materialism, scientism (as a philosophy of value which holds generally that facts point to evaluations), and optimism. Carried out consistently these would refute each other at crucial points, but together they have effectively strengthened man's conviction that he knows the good, that the mastery of nature gives him the power to achieve it, and that he possesses a stature big enough, by himself, to attain it" (p. 18). The Spann volume, while somewhat dated and uneven, contains much material still relevant to our study.

While the name was coined in the nineteenth century, the idea is much older. Machiavelli's *The Prince*—that much maligned, much misunderstood, and much distorted volume—was an earlier example of the spirit of secularism beginning to be systematized. More than two millennia earlier still Isaiah had recorded God's complaint that the people were taking a post-retirement-party attitude toward him:

> This people draw near with their mouth
> and honor me with their lips,

(they had no objection to saying a few kind words to the *emeritus* god)

> while their hearts are far from me,
> and their fear of me is a commandment of men
> learned by rote (Isaiah 29:13).

Secularism is very old.

Secularism is also very much alive. "Its nature is neither to affirm nor to deny religious faith, but to live indifferently to it." [5] e e cummings speaks of certain Cambridge ladies who believe in Longfellow and Christ, "both dead." That is a fair representation of a type of secularism, except that the secularist probably would not bother to announce the death. He does not care that much. Secularism is an

[5] *The Christian Faith and Secularism*, p. 11.

enacted atheism, an atheism in act. Secularism is therefore no respecter of philosophies. Obviously it may be found among those systems of thought which openly and often honestly deny or defy God. It may also be found among the pious.

II

Let us look at some places in our society, only a few of many, where secularism is to be found.

It is to be found in the public schools.

I believe in the free public schools. I believe it important that they be free, free from ideological pressure groups, whether political or religious. I believe it important that they be public, contributing to the welfare and serving the needs of the entire community, not of some racial segment, intellectual caste, or vocational fragment thereof. I believe it important that they be schools where young minds are stretched, old horizons pushed back, and new problems faced. I shall have more to say in chapter four about some of the insidious, invidious, and cynical threats against the very life of the public schools.

I am also glad, as a citizen and as a Christian, that the schools have been defrocked by the Supreme Court, that they are no longer either expected or permitted to function as a primary school version of required chapel. This does not mean that our children should not learn these prayers and Scripture. It means merely that it is not the public school's task to make up for parental and parochial neglect. Now the school can get on with its job, which is education.

I believe in the free public school, but I have a lover's quarrel with her. I remind her that some of us who, on religious grounds, will fight to protect her neutrality will insist that she protect it too. I remind her that the bigoted religion of secularism can be taught by silence. I remind her that those who do not believe in God have no more right to use her curriculum or her subtle influence to forward their sectarian views than I do. The religion of irreligion is still a religion of sorts, and it has been defrocked too. I remind her that the "anticlerical" Supreme Court has stated explicitly that teaching *about* religion is not illegal; and I remind her, as ungently as I can, that her administrators and curricular experts have shown singularly little imagination and insight in following up on that hint, for all the modern testing techniques, improved math, and team teaching about which they boast. Nationally prominent Court tests of two decades ago can no longer be the excuse for not engaging in nationally significant experiments in this matter, if we have the nerve and the will. We surely have the skill.

The danger is not in what the Supreme Court has done to the public school. The danger is in the inference we may mistakenly draw from this. It is constitutionally necessary to prohibit obligatory public prayers in the public school. This is quite proper in a necessarily secularized public school. What is not proper is to conclude that therefore God is dead.[6]

This, however, will be the inference unless the churches stop acting like secular institutions. We have criticized the schools for being "godless"—which they are not—but then have sat on our own weekday hands in order to cover up our neglect of our own educational task. But the neglect cannot be concealed. We badly need to give serious study, in many places, to the possibility of bold, new experiments in weekday education. Perhaps we could set up systematic programs of teaching by paid and qualified teachers on church property, outside of school hours. The secular public school harbors within its very nature a danger, but the danger could be an opportunity.

The weighted hand of secularism rests upon our lives, corporate and individual, at many points besides in the public school. We can act like atheists even while invoking the name of God. In a survey such as this these points can only be mentioned without being spelled out: in the family, in the nation, in the family of nations; in the terrible and often aimless activism of the churches, through which St. Vitus Dance the honest outsider could legitimately conclude that we think the whole thing depends upon us and that there is no "God with us" at all; through our mania for technological superiority, won at the price of moral mediocrity; through the face-

---

[6] This sentence is neither a reference to nor a condemnation of the various so-called "God is dead" theologians much in prominence these days.

less, card-punched skill through which we are capable of computing all things except what it means to be human in the twentieth century.

III

The analysis and criticism of secularism are important because *secularism is probably ethical religion's primary rival,* at least in the Western world. That is why I have chosen to commence this volume with a summary analysis of secularism.

As we approach now the task of trying more precisely to evaluate rather than describe it, let it be clearly understood that much commonly called secular should be approached in an appreciative, even in a grateful, spirit. Much that is worthy and of good report has come into the common inheritance through the efforts of men who are frankly and simply uninterested in what we call religious values but what they call religious illusions. This is being dramatized in the civil rights movement. Some of its leaders, like Martin Luther King, are men of faith and account for their works on that basis. Others could hardly care less. I have learned that whatever questions I may have about their doctrine, those questions do not apply to their devotion. It may be that they live far beyond their little creed, but they have forced the shamefaced awareness that some of us live far behind our big one. Other secularists in science, in government, in the public schools have a devotion for truth, a passion for inquiry, a readiness for service, and a concern for persons from whom we have much to learn. We should not excoriate them until we can at least equal them.

Nevertheless the Christian faith has an inevitable quarrel with secularism. Theologically its root sin is its belief in salvation by works. Man's sweat earns his bread, but it cannot quench his thirst—his thirst for forgiveness and wholeness, for direction and redirection, for meaning and love. We dare not become testy about this. If another thinks he can live by bread alone or achieve by himself alone, the most seemly reply is, "Perhaps so, but I cannot, and I cannot recall anyone who has." The secularist has a right to his quasi-credal illusions. They collide, however, with the Christian faith. Let there be no mistake about that.

It needs also to be suggested cautiously that secularism is lacking in humility. One of the meanings of the word *saeculum,* from which the word secular is derived, is: one age among many, or once in an age. Contemporary secularism, however, treats this age as the whole. James A. Pike states it with vivid homeliness when he writes, "Secularism means 'this ageism,' means 'this-is-all-there-is-ism';—it means 'there-ain't-any-more-ism.' That's it: you've had it." [7] I have tried to make it clear that much in this age should be approached with appreciation and appropriated with joy. However history did not begin with the

[7] Franklin H. Littell, ed., *Sermons to Intellectuals* (New York: The Macmillan Company, 1963), p. 108.

microscope, and progress will not end with the "Great Society." Secularism has a valid tale to tell, but it is not the whole story. "The secular world," as Samuel H. Miller has aptly suggested, "is merely . . . the world waiting for its full meaning."[8] That meaning has not yet been realized, however; nor, on secularism's terms, is it likely to be.

This critique of secularism cannot conclude without a word to the church doing the criticizing. A mark of the secular age is that in it man "is not hostile to religion, or even concerned. He simply does not raise the religious question at all, not even in church."[9] So my concern is not that the Christian gospel has become secularized by our culture. That is the fate of many a great idea. Men will adopt it, adapt it, change it, misinterpret or misuse it. I am concerned that the Christian gospel is being secularized by the church. I am concerned lest the church become as secular, as cut off from its original sources, as the culture against which she stands as conscience. I am concerned that the Christian church continue faithfully in her Lord's vineyard, wherever others may choose to plant or try to reap. I am concerned lest the church, in her casual reading of the parable of the Good Samaritan, should herself cease to be one. The world can continue to live on the Lord's teachings without acknowledging

[8] *The Dilemma of Modern Belief*, p. 91.

[9] Quoted in Gabriel Vahanian, *The Death of God* (New York: George Braziller, 1961), p. 148.

him as Lord, but the church owns no such right, for he is not chosen by us but given to us. The church is by definition a fellowship of followers "rooted and grounded" in him and planted by Providence for the specific purpose of "growing up unto him in all things."

Thus it is that when creeds collide, each may come to understand itself and the other the more. That is at least one of the purposes of this book.

2

HUMANISM—WHICH KIND?

A wise thinker once replied to a question about how his thought was to be labeled by saying, "You can call me anything you like so long as I may define the terms." As we come to the difficult task of defining the term "humanism," that remark is wise and apropos. Who is a humanist? I am perfectly willing, indeed quite eager, to affirm that I am a humanist if I may define the word. Few presumptions are more irritating than the arrogant, unhistorical, provincial way some men have purloined, perverted, and attempted to monopolize this word. They have spoken of "humanism" and "religion" as if they were antonyms. I hold, on the contrary, that one cannot be a Christian, really and fully, without being a humanist. So the question apparently is, which kind?

I

Classic humanism arose from the rediscovery of human values as set forth and embodied in the human documents of ancient Greece and recovered during the Middle Ages. The phenomenon began in the fourteenth century with Pétrarch (1304-1374), an Italian priest. It came to flower during the Renaissance when, after centuries of preoccupation with God, the center stage of history began to be occupied by man. It was easier, however, to gain a name for this movement of the mind than it was to attach to it any single and unitary definition.

The thing itself had existed without a name for two thousand years before that. In the Athens of the fifth century B.C., thinkers began to turn from a study of the material world to a consideration of the mind of man. This turning, or turning upward, to human values was humanism without the label. Protagoras (c. 490–after 421 B.C.) gave it its essential statement, for then and for now, with his maxim about man as the measure of all things—a maxim, as we shall see, so nearly right yet so clearly wrong from a Christian perspective.

Humanism, as understood classically, was a liberating force (as we also observed in chapter one of secularization in our time); it freed man to take himself seriously. It ranged his unfettered, mobile, and creative intelligence against all that would bind his mind or put leg irons on his spirit. It produced great works of art in poetry and painting, in architecture and music. Rodin's statue "The Thinker" is a modern production, but in spirit it was carved from the ancient granite of humanism. Scholarship became a way of life. Cathedrals were seen as marking not only the glory of God but also the ingenuity of man.

Of direct interest to persons of religion is the fact that in the beginning most humanists were churchmen, if only because most education was in their hands and for their benefit. We have already mentioned Pétrarch, who was a priest. John Colet (1467?-1519) in England is also worthy of note, with his warning, so needed today, against the arrogance, rashness, and pride of presuming to define everything, thus excising much of the mystery and wonder from life. Philipp Melanchthon (1497-1560), Luther's younger colleague in the German Reformation, was called at the age of twenty-one to the chair of Greek at Wittenberg. John Calvin (1509-1564) was a humanist before he was a theologian.[1] In Holland, Erasmus, that ceaseless traveler, was letting his mind also roam over the vast universe of the truth of God in the lives of men. He could not quite bring himself to break with the church, although he criticized her stringently. Not without justi-

[1] Cf. Lynn Harold Hough, *The Christian Criticism of Life* (Nashville: Abingdon-Cokesbury Press, 1941), p. 238.

fication has he been called "the greatest of the Humanists." [2]

One very direct and continuing consequence in the life
of the church was what happened to the Scriptures under
the aegis and impetus of the humanists. Once you have
turned loose the mind of man, you have no way of knowing
where it will come down to examine and criticize, to
cleanse and restore. Once men had learned that the
writings of Aristotle and the dialogues of Plato could be
studied, dissected, and recovered, it was no great surprise
that they turned with a like eagerness—serious, sustained,
and unafraid of the consequences—to the writings they
had long called holy. The original languages were studied;
the ancient presuppositions were examined; cultures buried
beneath the settled debris of the ages were literally un-
earthed. Sentences were parsed; paragraphs were compared;
books were studied in relation to their beginning setting
and checked against other contemporary documents; their
writers and lead characters, from Isaiah to Paul and back
again, became live figures with foibles, hopes, and aspira-
tions. The result was that the Holy Bible was seen to be,
not less holy for being human, but more holy, and more
authentic.

The movement was not without its defects. It tended to
exalt erudition for its own sake, thus contributing to the
modern heresy that knowledge in itself is moral. Its

[2] *Encyclopedia of Religion and Ethics,* VI, 835b.

devotion to style sometimes degenerated into the merely stylistic, thus contributing to the excesses of Romanticism which occasionally asked only, *Is it beautiful?* while neglecting another classic question, *Is it true?* These defects, however, were but the excess of its virtues which, on balance, are weightier than its weaknesses. Humanism made man's mind a fitter instrument, gave his spirit a more capacious living space, and surrounded him with those graces and beauties which made him at once gentler and stronger—in short, more human.

II

There is another humanism less humane. It is called, variously, naturalistic humanism, scientific humanism, or (in Julian Huxley's phrase) evolutionary humanism. If the early humanism of the Greeks was born when men turned from a study of the elements to a contemplation of man, the modern variety can largely be understood as a turn back again to the study of things. Not without reason has this modern regression been called an "inhuman humanism." [3] The phrase "inhuman humanism" is not so much a judgment of its value as it is a description of its interests.

Webster's Third, the Peck's Bad Boy of modern usage, defines this newer, lesser humanism as follows: "a doctrine,

---

[3] See Henri de Lubac, *The Drama of Atheist Humanism* (New York: The World Publishing Company, 1963), p. 6; also Jacques Maritain, *True Humanism* (New York: Charles Scribner's Sons, 1939), p. 20.

set of attitudes, or way of life centered upon human interests or values." Thus far, fairly good, although the significance of that word *doctrine* should not be missed. An elaborating definition continues: "rejects supernaturalism, regards man as a natural object, and asserts . . . his capacity to achieve self-realization through the use of reason and scientific method."

Very little is wrong with humanism so defined, but that little is fatal, literally and philosophically. Consider, for instance, the assertion being made here that man is "a natural object." That is true. Few things are more productive of a salutary sense of humility than an accurate enumeration of the pitiful little list of chemicals which, in sum and in combination, go to make up a human body. Add to that the fact that one malfunctioning gland can reduce a genius to a blithering blob of almost inanimate idiocy, and you have a very sobering picture of man as an object of nature.

Note, however, who makes this observation. Is it the chemicals themselves, suddenly quickened into intelligence? Is it the gland in some grand moment of superglandular insight? No, it is *a man* who, though a bag of bones and an array of chemicals, must transcend them both in order to write about them at all. Pascal may be permitted his humbling conceit that man "is a thinking reed" so long as we remember that a reed, the product of nature, does not think at all. Since this is so, it is difficult to fathom how the otherwise brilliant Julian Huxley could conclude, with no sense of shock or humor or incongruity, that "the mindless universe has generated mind." [4]

It is, then, quite legitimate to say that man is a part of nature. It is not quite legitimate to say that man is *merely* a part of nature. This is a little like saying that one can understand everything in *Romeo and Juliet* by a study of sexual jealousy among mating otters. About the only important elements such an analysis would miss would be the hero, the heroine, the plot, and the speeches. [5]

III

It will be helpful in bringing naturalistic humanism into focus if we take a brief, critical look at Julian Huxley, probably its most brilliant and able representative. He is a biologist of widely recognized credentials and accomplishments. In his volume *Religion Without Revelation* he states, "The basic postulate of evolutionary humanism is that mental and spiritual forces . . . do have operative effect, and are indeed of decisive importance in the highly practical business of working out human destiny; and . . . *they are not* supernatural, not *outside man but within him*." [6] (Italics mine.) This is Protagoras with

[4] *Knowledge, Morality, and Destiny* (Mentor ed.; New York: The New American Library, 1957), p. 224.

[5] Cf. *The Secular Promise*, p. 63.

[6] (Mentor ed.; New York: The New American Library, [1957] 1958), p. 195.

a British accent and a microscope: man the measure of all
things.

It would be difficult to improve upon or take issue with
his statement about belief and faith. He points out that
"though by their nature they include a nonrational element, (they) need not be either irrational or anti-rational,
unscientific or anti-scientific." [7]

Huxley intends no basic conflict between science and
religion: "Between scientific knowledge and certain religious systems, yes: but between science as an increasing
knowledge of nature and religion as a social organ concerned with destiny, no." [8] Although Mr. Huxley *intends*
no such conflict, the peace terms are, it seems to me,
unconditional surrender on the part of religion.

I would want to contend that he is right for the wrong
reason. There is no collision of science with religion
because the two are traveling on different courses. Science
deals with measurable fact; religion with immeasurable.
Science is a question-asking device about the quantitative;
religion is a question-asking device about the qualitative.
(Religion has sometimes, erroneously, been presented as an
answer-giving device and has thus fallen into the trap of
"answering" questions few are asking.) Huxley rejects
these distinctions. Thus the conflict he wishes to avoid is
inevitable.

Religionists have been severely and justly attacked for

[7] *Knowledge, Morality, and Destiny*, pp. 90-91.
[8] *Ibid.*, p. 261.

making pronouncements about scientific matters beyond their ken or competence: how the world was created; whether man can produce life. Huxley, however, observes little such restraint himself. Here is a clear example of the collision course he steers: "Evolutionary biology makes it clear that the developed human personality is, in a strictly scientific sense, the highest product of the cosmic process of which we have any knowledge." [9] Hold! Biology possesses no instrument with which even to *recognize* personality let alone to judge its value. I draw that conclusion not on the basis of my definition of personality but on the basis of his. The personality, he says, is "a spiritual and mental construction." [10] Here we have a wondrous thing indeed: a biological science allegedly able to detect spiritual value. Perhaps Mr. Huxley meant to write "individuality" rather than "personality." This would have been somewhat more defensible and in any case verifiable. If he did mean that, he should have written that. If on the other hand he meant what he wrote—and I cannot escape the conclusion that he did—then he is guilty of the kind of credulity and carelessness which he rightly disdains and usually avoids.

The sum of the matter, as I see it, is this: Science does a good job in describing how a molecule acts and reacts. It even does quite well in identifying many of the complexities that make up a man. When, however, it moves from describing my action to evaluating my aspira-

[9] *Religion Without Revelation*, p. 194.
[10] *Ibid.*, p. 201.

tion—when, that is, it moves into the realm of values—it moves too far. Stated philosophically the same thing would be said thus: As a method it is fine; as a metaphysic it is futile. To quote Mr. Huxley himself, "a biologist cannot answer a question framed in terms of purpose." [11]

At this point the eminent biologist seems to me either not quite radical enough or not quite honest enough. (I rather think it is the former.) Instead of taking such pains to insist that a science-religion conflict is avoidable or at least regrettable, he should state that the two in fact collide when *either* gets out of orbit. Instead of bringing God back in just before the final philosophical curtain, he should admit that what he means by God bears no important resemblance to what religion means by it.[12] Even on such a vital matter as whether or what God is, honest irreconcilables are preferable to doctored resemblances. It is quite permissible for Mr. Huxley to define terms as he likes. But in this case it is also quite deceptive. For my intellectual money it is not that he is too radical; it is that he is not radical enough.

I would finally assert that scientific humanism fails to consider all the data, surprisingly enough. Let me sum it in an epigram: The most significant fact about science is

[11] *Knowledge, Morality, and Destiny*, p. 196.

[12] "The word 'God' formulates in one single term and concept various features of man's experiences, such as sacredness, transcendent significance, permanence, ultimacy, personal authority (including its functions such as responsibility and loving care as well as justice and compulsion), and power." *Ibid.*, p. 243.

the scientist. Let him construct a microscope and study natural life. Let there be no restrictions—absolutely none —on his search for data. If he is able to produce life in a test tube, then as a Christian humanist I say, "May God be praised!" To take another instance, the vast reaches and intricate calculations of astronomy are literally marvels to behold. For me a greater marvel is the astronomer himself, who designs the telescope, makes the calculations, and builds the science. He himself is an important but too often ignored part of the data. Any evaluation of scientific humanism must stand or fall on the basis of the method's capacity or lack of capacity to account for and understand the scientific humanist.

As a Christian humanist I ask my scientific friends to ponder that fact. The method to which the scientist is so rightly and so fruitfully committed is not able to weigh the significance of the man employing the method. But the man himself can. My contention is that, if he does, both the man and his science will be to that degree more fully human. Man is not the measure of all things. He is the measurer.

It is very clear, quite beyond what I have written here, that we are all richly indebted to scientific humanism. Its usual humble unwillingness to generalize beyond the allowable limits of the data is alone a splendid gift to mankind. I could hope to observe more of it in more conventionally religious quarters. Its ceaseless search for new light on old facts, its complete readiness to discard everything and start over if that is what is required, its restless technological ingenuity—these have literally changed the face of the earth and lightened the burdens of the inhabitants thereof. With humanism as a tactic, Christianity has no quarrel. With humanism as a creed, a collision is unavoidable.

The Christian church has, in my judgment, come perilously close to losing its heritage of authentic humanism. It has been too quick to assume that humanism is a bad word just because it is sometimes used badly. It has been too timid to declare its kinship with other thoughtful affirmations of what is genuinely humane simply because those other affirmations bear a strange or another label.

That label may be, for example, "sociology." Some of its practitioners labor to help us understand the Negro matriarchies of the inner city. The church may thereby be prevented from approving the ignorant politician's scream that we do not want any of *our* tax money squandered to support illegitimate children. Christian humanists will not insist that such sociology be "Christianized." Rather, they will recognize such data, raw and unsettling though they may be, as capable of contributing to the authentically humane values for which both humanisms should stand.

When we fail to recognize the value of these other humanisms, perhaps it is a case of bad memory. For the heart of our creed is that God himself valued human life with such utter seriousness that he clothed himself in Christ to share it.[18] That kind of humanism or even one simply open to that possibility—in any century or culture, under any name or sign—it is our duty to protect and our privilege to proclaim.

[18] "Faith is nothing other than the knowledge that *God* thinks us men to be of utmost importance. This 'humanism' is implied in God's incarnation in Jesus Christ, and to reject this humanism would be nothing less than to reject Christ." Emil Brunner, *Dogmatics* (3 vols.; Philadelphia: The Westminster Press, 1960), III, 174. Paul M. Van Buren has commented on the same fact when, from his own peculiar perspective, he writes, "The Christian is nothing if not one who is concerned for man, and his 'humanism' is defined by the history of that man [the reference is to Jesus Christ] and his strange but human freedom, which has become contagious." See *The Secular Meaning of the Gospel* (New York: The Macmillan Company, 1963), p. 160.

3

COMMUNISM—WHAT'S NOT RIGHT ABOUT THE LEFT?

I begin this chapter on communism by identifying four presuppositions. They are legitimately debatable among fair-minded men. They are also, in my judgment, defensible. In any case what follows here will make more sense if the reader takes into account the following assumptions.

1. I assume that it is increasingly difficult to attach to the word "communism" (or its cognates) any one definition which will be adequate for all times, places, and situations. Is the reference to an economic system, to a political organization, to a social theory? Does one mean

Chinese communism or Yugoslavian? The writings of Marx or Lenin? The communism of Khrushchev or that of Stalin? If the latter, then which Stalin: the one his countrymen respected in life or the one they reviled in death? When one says "communist," he has not said much unless he is able to supply and willing to examine a context, a modifier, or an elaboration.

2. My second assumption, a correlate of the first, is that people who ignore these nuances and distinctions in "interpreting" communism are liable to lead us badly astray. Those who suppose that communism is one vast, monolithic, unchanging structure and strategy from the 1840's to the 1960's simply have made an insufficiently critical study of the movement. They are usually using the word as a term of opprobrium but not as an instrument of description. That just does not happen to be an exercise in which I am particularly interested.

3. My third assumption is that when we collate what Communists think and do and what we think and do, we should compare their best with our best and contrast their worst with our worst. It is easy to score points by placing what Khrushchev said in a fit of temper alongside what Jefferson said in a moment of wisdom. Any freshman debater knows, and maybe employs, that trick. Our purpose, however, is illumination and understanding, not recrimination and undercutting.

4. My fourth assumption is that, nevertheless, in studying

communism we should make a manifest distinction between its claims and its conduct. If what the Soviet
constitution provides is stoned to death by what the
Soviet courts permit, we should face and state that fact
clearly and candidly. This implies, however, the readiness
to recognize the same kind of bifurcation when it occurs
in our national and international life: what is voted in the
chambers of the Senate does not always exactly correspond
with what is violated in the streets of Selma.

With these assumptions out in the open, then, let us
proceed to examine another of the live creeds with which
Christianity collides.

I

Karl Marx was born in Tréves, Prussia, on May 5, 1818.
His father, a lawyer, was Jewish by birth but Christian
by profession. The younger Marx studied at the universities
of Bonn, Berlin, and Jena. The details of his theory are
fairly well known or, if not known, readily ascertainable
by consulting any basic text in political philosophy or
economics. In a study such as this, the most we can
justifiably do is provide the roughest of summaries.

Marx was not an especially original economist. Many
of his main ideas were derived from the classical economists
of the early capitalist period, notably Adam Smith. According to Marx the fundamental feature of all civilizations is
the system by which people produce material goods. The
so-called values of civilization—religion, art, philosophy

—are little more than superstructures built on top of the economic order. The power structure of any civilization will attempt to justify and perpetuate possession of that power. Religion is especially guilty here, says Marx—hence the familiar but hardly original charge that religion is the opiate of the people. The only way in which justice can be achieved, the argument continues, is by the abolition of all social-economic classes all over the world. Workers must unite to accelerate this irresistible process. This, in the sparsest of detail, is the revolutionary idea which Marx manumitted upon an unready and unsuspecting world.[1]

Julian Huxley has stated its philosophical motifs in the following:

The dominant idea-system of the non-West, the system of Marxism and dialectical materialism, began by taking over the emerging idea of process and the historical outlook from Hegel and Darwin. It then took the idea of scientific method from the Western world, the materialist outlook from physical science and technology, and the economic and class outlook (but not the individualist outlook) from the social structure of the nineteenth-century West. In so doing, Marxism accomplished a curious feat: it took over the basic dualism of Western European thought, but then proceeded to transform it into

[1] Cf. the essay "Rival Secular Faiths" by Wilhelm Pauck in *Man's Disorder and God's Design* (5 vols.; New York: Harper and Brothers, 1948), II, 37 ff. Here in a few paragraphs (pp. 43-45) is an extraordinarily succinct and able summary of the essence of Marxism.

a phony monism, a sham unitary system, by denying validity
to one of its two components, namely, the mental aspect.[2]

The bomb was constructed by Marx, but the fuse was
attached and later lighted by Lenin. Lenin was but a
teen-ager when Marx died. His very earliest writings as a
young man had begun to translate the harmless-sounding
ideas of his German master into the tough, strident tones
of an upheaval which was to leave his native Russia
torn, bleeding, and breathless—yet, after a space, poised
for conquest. Take this sample, as surly as it is timely:

The scientific concept "dictatorship" means nothing more or
less than unrestricted power, absolutely unimpeded by laws
or regulations and resting directly upon force. *This* is the
meaning of the concept "dictatorship" and *nothing else*. Keep
this well in mind.[3]

Thus the prose of a German philosopher became the
powder of a Russian revolution.

It has by now become rather fashionable to observe
that what the present-day Soviet system passes off as
Marxism would hardly be recognized by its founder as his
legitimate intellectual child. This is in part what I had in
mind when I referred earlier to the difficulty of attaching
any unitary definition to the word "Communist." If one
could arrange some intercontinental version of the tele-

[2] *Knowledge, Morality, and Destiny,* pp. 232-33.
[3] Lenin, *Selected Works,* VII, 123, 254.

vision show "To Tell the Truth," one would hardly know what to expect at the request, "Will the real Marxist please stand up?" "Lenin 'adjusted' Marxism to suit his purpose; in the process he strangled it."[4] Stalin in turn adjusted Leninism; Khrushchev twisted Stalinism; now Khrushchev himself is a cipher wrapped in silence. It is estimated that at least twenty countries now have two mutually hostile Communist parties devoting much of their energies to fighting each other.[5] Thus *The New York Times* observes with only slight exaggeration that ironically, "the outstanding feature of Marxists today is their utter indifference to, and complete ignorance of—Marxism."[6]

In the United States the Communist party has had its membership ups and downs, mostly downs. Even in one of its two periods of most rapid growth, namely, the Great Depression of the 1930's, the Communists themselves were complaining that they were losing members as rapidly as they had gained them.[7] Peak membership was probably reached in 1949 in conjunction with the Wallace presidential campaign. Reliable estimates indicate that party rolls

[4] Robert Strausz-Hupe, "Between the Ideal and the Ideology," *The Saturday Review* (June 12, 1965), p. 38. Cf. on this point Bertram D. Wolfe's *Marxism: 100 Years in the Life of a Doctrine* (New York: The Dial Press, 1965).

[5] Cf. Zbigniew Brzezinski, "Reassessing Communism," *motive* (January, 1966), p. 35.

[6] "The Twentieth Century Began in 1945," *The New York Times Magazine* (May 2, 1965), p. 80.

[7] Cf. S. Tsirul, *The Practice of Bolshevik Self-Criticism* (New York Central Committee CPUSA, 1932), p. 17.

may have contained as many as seventy-five to eighty
thousand members. By the 1960's this number is judged
to have shrunk to between five and twenty thousand.[8]
Even former Ambassador to Russia George F. Kennan,
who was so "soft on communism" that they threw him out
of the country for allegedly anti-Soviet remarks in 1952,
has recently written of the American Communist party:

Today it is a tiny and pathetic little band of people embracing,
I suppose, not much more than five thousand members, if that,
or something less than one hundredth part of one percent of
our adult population. It is no exaggeration to say that the influence of the American Communist Party today in our society
is negligible. If you were to comb the country, you would have
a hard time finding a less influential group.[9]

The simple fact is that, despite prodigious and continuing
efforts to sell itself on the part of the American Communist
party, the vast majority of Americans are not buying.

Some inroads were made for a time, however, in parts
of the American labor movement. Yet as the Overstreets
point out in their excellent, documented study, the CIO,
a major communist target from the mid-thirties, had by
the late forties painfully identified those unions under
Marxist influence and had expelled them from the organiza-

[8] Cf. *The Profile of Communism*, ed. and rev. Moshe Decter (New
York: Collier Books, 1961).

[9] "The Right Way to Counter Communism," *Presbyterian Life* (July
15, 1965), p. 7.

tion. Thus, "organized labor in America has gone far toward making every factory a fortress against Communism."[10]

Likewise the American Negro, whose compacted woes would seem to have made him especially vulnerable to the wiles of Marxist utopian promises, has instead tenaciously insisted upon more democracy, not less. Efforts to win the American Negro represent one of communism's most signal failures.

Such resistance forced the Communist party in the United States to adopt a technique as old as the Trojan horse, namely, the Front organization. Selecting and exploiting issues in which decent, idealistic, and sometimes naive Americans were interested anyway, controlling policy and direction by means of a small ingroup, the party had more success through covert strategy than it had had through open appeal. When we were at war, when Russians were our allies, it was no great trick to get Americans to join organizations like the National Council of American-Soviet Friendship, Inc., or to persuade prominent citizens to associate their names with its activities. This particular organization was thus able to tie in such notables as Senators Green, McKellar and Pepper; Governor Leverett Saltonstall; General Eisenhower. This does not mean that General Eisenhower was interested in forwarding com-

[10] Harry and Bonaro Overstreet, *What We Must Know About Communism* (New York: W. W. Norton & Company, 1958), p. 202.

munism but rather that communism was intent upon exploiting General Eisenhower.

The biggest factor in assessing the American scene, however, is that Mr. Marx badly miscalculated in his prophecies about the decadence, resolution, and adaptability of capitalism. Doctrinaire Marxists continue to predict that capitalism will fall of its own dead weight. Nevertheless free enterprise also continues at once more free and more enterprising than the gloomy German believed possible. The needed reforms, which Marx thought could be accomplished only by violence, have in large part been brought about mostly by volition. Laws, taxes, bargaining tables, good faith, and good will—these have made the supposedly inevitable revolution as useless as a screen door on a submarine.

II

As we come to the task of evaluating this multiform phenomenon known as communism, it may be well to state still another of my presuppositions, omitted earlier because it has greater bearing here. That is, I presuppose that we may expect to find, upon examination, that communism is a medley of truth and falsehood, good and evil, and a mixture of all four. It may be permissible, for the purposes of polemic or campaign oratory, to assume the system is all false and evil or all true and good, depending upon where one stands. That way of seeing it or saying it, however, hardly contributes to clarity, charity, or understanding. Those who want a sheep and goats division of the world into West and East will hardly be staisfied by what follows here.

The eminent Cambridge historian, Herbert Butterfield, has given it as his judgment that

The Marxists are right when they assume that a member of a certain social class, even if he is unselfish, is liable to be limited in his outlook by the fact that he sees things from the platform of that social class.[11]

The peaceful form which the Industrial Revolution has taken in much of the West has nevertheless not brought about its changes entirely voluntarily. What is good for General Motors may be good for the country, but the general consensus is that General Motors is scarcely the best judge. So it is too with laboring people, with white people, with church people, with vested interested groups of all kinds. Part of the genius of democracy is the way in which it provides ready-made structures to adjudicate the disputes of such groups. Those who object to the social pressure exerted by "demonstrations" of various kinds fail to realize that few privileged groups give up their privileges voluntarily. Indeed such objections themselves are sometimes the clearest possible indication that Marx was correct here.

[11] *Christianity and History* (New York: Fontana Books, 1952), p. 118.

On the negative side a list of things not right about the left would have to include at least the following:

1. The Marxist uses the word *democracy* to mean government *for* the people. By ignoring the crucial preposition *of*, he can write off free elections as unnecessary; by chopping off the crucial preposition *by*, he can assume that "Big Brother" knows what is best for the little brothers who make up the general populace. Thus the curtained phrase "People's Democracy" takes seriously neither the people nor democracy.

2. When Lenin says that "Religion is a kind of spiritual gin," [12] he fails to recognize that though this is sometimes true, what he substitutes for the gin of religion is the poison of idolatry. Moreover the idolatry of communism is many times worse and infinitely more dangerous than its atheism. It is at this point that we confront the description of communism as a religious entity, a description so perplexing to so many. Anything that summons a man's unqualified allegiance—as communism does for many of its adherents—has about it in some form a religious quality. In a world of rational men honest atheism is a possible option about which they may argue and decide. But whereas the atheist may be honest, the idolator is presumptuous.

3. Another thing not right about the left is its single theory "explanation" of man and his history, a so-called explanation in economic terms. Historians have long since

[12] *Selected Works*, IX, 68.

disposed of the great man theory of history. Certainly you cannot understand the Second World War without taking account of Churchill, but you must take account of a great deal else besides. The Marxist, however, stubbornly clings to his "great economics" theory of history. Certainly you cannot understand the long struggle called human history unless you take account of what man produces, what he does with what he produces, and how. Nevertheless, that does not exhaust the question of the meaning of history. It only begs it.

I would contend that the half-truths of communism are more dangerous than its blatant errors. I can join the Marxist in his observation that history is economically conditioned, that class conflict is real, and that man may be corrupted by his propertied selfishness. I cannot join the Marxist in his conclusion that *therefore* history is economically *determined,* that conflict can itself seek out social solutions, or that if we remove the lollipops men will cease to crave candy.

III

It remains for us to inquire—since clearly this is a creed which collides with the Christian one—what should be the stance of Christians vis-à-vis communism.

I would suggest, first, that we should remember there are Christians behind the various Marxian curtains that divide our world. It ill behooves us, who live in a free land, blithely to assume that we know quite certainly how we would act if we lived there instead of here. No one of us can quite conceive just what it means to try to be a Christian in a Marxist country. *The Christian church is the one remaining genuinely international community in a world whose peoples are sinfully divided from each other.* When, therefore, misguided Christians oppose international conferences and conversations involving Christians from behind the Iron Curtain, they come perilously close to an unforgivable sin. They have divided brother from brother, sapping the power of each to love and serve the other.

I would propose, secondly, that we examine our own national policies and practices. Is it possible that Marxian doctrine has insinuated itself into our midst under terribly respectable or even patriotic-sounding names? The doctrine that the end justifies the means—how different is this from the rationalizations that led us to unleash atomic destruction upon Japan? The end, peace, was good, we said, so damn the damned means. One important difference, of course, is that this corrupt doctrine is for the Communist a constant and unvarying strategy, whereas for us it has been an infrequent and intermittent extremity, but we should at least identify and admit the extremity. The doctrine of dialectical materialism—ours perhaps is not dialectical, just practical—"refrigerator-cum-television materialism" as it has been called.[13] Is it really *that* different

[13] Helmut Thielicke, *The Freedom of the Christian Man,* trans. John W. Doberstein (New York: Harper & Row, 1963), p. 113.

from the Marxist form which we so roundly, and sometimes self-righteously, condemn? Again, the theory of class conflict, which is surely "an intellectual alibi for the collective will to power" [14]—is it possible that its Western, Americanized, acceptable form is the despicable pseudo-patriotism, "My country right or wrong"? It may be that in order to understand and withstand communism, we need a good stiff dose of *this* kind of anticommunism, the kind which is ready to recognize the wretch in both Washington and Warsaw. The world will take small notice of our cries that Marxism is sick unless we are also willing to say, "Democratic Physician, heal thyself!"

Suppose, just suppose, that we should awake tomorrow morning to find that the Iron Curtain has been dismantled.[15] Students could begin enrolling in Russian universities. My Christian Chinese friend, David Kwante Ling, could come to America and preach from my pulpit. Businessmen and farmers could exchange goods, ideas, and prosperity. American politicians would not have to "stand up to" anybody, and Russian politicians could smile simply because they were happy, not because they were trying to bewitch or confuse us.

Suppose all this. Now my questions are: What, that we most surely believe, would we have to say to the world? to the communist world? to ourselves? What are *we*

[14] *Ibid.*, p. 100.
[15] I am indebted to Thielicke, *ibid.*, p. 109, for the form of this idea although not, of course, for my development of it.

ultimately committed to? How eager are we to share it?
to sacrifice for it? What do we really know about the
minds and hearts of men whose friendship and coopera-
tion we say we would like to win? What commends our
way to them? What divides our way from them?

Is it not clear that much of what we would want to say to
them would have first to be addressed to ourselves? Is
it not sure that in order to be candidly critical in the
councils of the nations we would have to be honestly
self-critical in our Congress, in our churches, in our cities
and towns, in our homes, and in our hearts?

Augustine once observed that a nation is an association
of reasonable beings united in a peaceful sharing of the
things they cherish; therefore, he added, to determine the
quality of a nation, you must consider what those things
are.[16]

What are the things we cherish, or ought to cherish?
Hidden in that question is the legitimate ground of conflict, the permanent ground of Judgment, and the ultimate
ground of hope.

[16] Cf. *The City of God* xix. 24.

4

WHAT'S WRONG ON THE RIGHT?

Before commencing the research for this book, I asked a librarian to secure for my use the back numbers of several magazines. They ranged from the liberal Roman Catholic publication *The Commonweal* to the conservative *National Review,* which describes itself as "a journal of fact and opinion" and which actually does a rather consistent job of distinguishing between fact and opinion.

As I began working through the articles, I discovered that some amateur editor had rewritten in the margins almost every one of them on the subject of the Radical Right. The following are some random words and phrases copied from those pencilled in the margins: "a smear article," "what rot," "nonsense," "good" (this in reaction to a reader's suggestion that the magazine in question ought to be burned), "the above is a traitorous article," "a lie and a smear," "an anti-American discourse," "this magazine is seditious."

I relate the foregoing because it enables me to make several related points rather quickly:

1. Dialogue—open, honest, respectful-of-the-other-person communication—is not probable with the radical, whether of the Left or of the Right. He is not interested in talking with you—only at you or past you. People who think with their adjectives have their intellectual slip showing, thus making well-dressed discourse unlikely.

2. The second thing to be learned from these pencilled "improvements" is that the real crime is not in being a liberal or a conservative but in questioning the rightist party line. An almost frighteningly lucid example of this is the manner in which William F. Buckley, Jr. has acquired the unearned dividend of the Right's anger. Buckley, editor of the aforementioned *National Review,* is almost Mr. Conservative himself. Nevertheless he has for some time been declaring that it is impossible to defend the *leadership* of the John Birch Society. Now, moving a step further, he has referred to the society's "paranoid and unpatriotic drivel." This has drawn from Billy James Hargis of the so-called Christian Crusade the judgment that "Buckley has committed suicide as far as his standing with anti-Communists in this country is con-

cerned. . . . His declaration of war on the John Birch
Society will ruin him."[1] Buckley is about as far to the
left as the tip end of the right wing of the American
eagle. If Buckley's authentic conservatism is subject to
such abuse, O Lord, who shall stand!

I am not, then, very optimistic about communicating
with the Radical Right in this chapter—and that by
their choice, not mine. I am rather concentrating upon fair-
minded America. I am addressing myself to responsible
people whether conservative or liberal. I direct my words
to those who believe in the free institutions of our society,
who honor the rules of straightforward debate, who respect
the right of an opponent to oppose, and who are willing
to put their case with that combination of passion and
impartiality through which evidence can be weighed,
decisions made, and freedom multiplied.

On these terms I shall ask and try to answer the
question, "What's wrong on the Right?" I propose to do
this by examining in some detail one organization among
many and one book among many and then making some
general observations about this complex movement as a
whole.

I

The subject organization is the John Birch Society.
The society arose out of a meeting called by Robert H.
Welch and eleven men invited by him, held in Indianap-

[1] *Christian Century* (August 25, 1965), p. 1028.

olis, Indiana, on December 8 and 9, 1958. Since membership rolls are apparently secret[2] and since no accounting
is made of dues or contributions, it is extremely difficult
to estimate the material strength of the group. It is
believed that the 1963 reported income was more than a
million dollars.[3] *The Chicago Daily News,* referring to
recent statements by Mr. Welch, indicates he "has about
80,000 followers in 5,000 chapters" and that "the society
. . . will spend between $5,000,000 and $6,000,000 in
1965—almost twice as much as the Republican National
Committee."[4] Mr. Welch from the beginning insisted
upon, and up until now has maintained, a completely
autocratic control of the organization, expelling local cells
or individual members according to his own lights.

The society is not a part of the "hate Right" about
which I have a bit more to say later in this chapter. By
and large its members, so far as they have been willing to
identify themselves, appear to be rather urbane, mostly
educated, quite successful people. Its directives to the
membership contain a number of references to the necessity
of courtesy and civility. The charge that the organization

[2] Cf. *The Radical Right,* ed. Daniel Bell (Rev. Anchor ed.; Garden City,
N. Y.: Doubleday & Company, 1964), p. 252. It was in an earlier edition
of this book, under the title *The New American Right,* that the term
"Radical Right" was coined in an essay by Seymour Martin Lipset.

[3] "What Is Extremism?" Pamphlet published by the American Jewish
Committee, p. 9.

[4] November 22, 1965, p. 7.

is antisemitic is based largely upon suspicion and upon guilt by association, both inadmissible evidence.

In a sixteen-page advertising supplement to the *Saint Louis Globe Democrat,* Welch says of membership in the society:

Merely being patriotic or anti-Communist is not sufficient qualification for membership. We must have associated with us, now and in the future, only men and women of good will, good conscience, and religious ideals. For we are striving to set an example, by dedication, integrity and purpose—in word and deed—which our children's children may follow without hesitation.[5]

That sounds like an irenic, gracious, and patriotic statement. Surely only the misanthrope or the Marxist himself could opt against it.

However, many have taken exception, and the critics I have in mind are neither haters of mankind nor Communists. Most striking of all is the growing list of disclaimers coming from those who count themselves conservatives. The list includes such names as these: Russell Kirk, who has been to the conservative academic world what Buckley is to the conservative journalistic

[5] November 1, 1964, back color cover. This supplement, which apparently appeared in several newspapers at about the same time, provides an interesting indication of the Society's financial capacities.

world; Barry Goldwater;[6] Senator Everett Dirksen, who
is a conservative—on some days at least. Apparently, then,
there is more to Mr. Welch's political candy than the
coating he is fond of quoting.

The trouble is that it is a good deal easier to describe
what the typical Bircher does not believe than what he
does, for the program is essentially negative, *anti*. Besides
communism, he is against United States membership in
the United Nations; against GATT (the General Agree-
ment on Trades and Tariffs); against the "useless and
costly NATO"; against "so-called defense spending" (even
although usually he also wants simultaneous increase of
military activity); against all foreign aid; against diplomatic relations with communist countries; against the National
Labor Relations Act, social security, the graduated income
tax, if not all income tax, the Rural Electrification Admini-
stration, forced integration[7]—and this is a *select* list of
his antipathies.

Even so it does not seem to me that the society is
drawing fire alone because of its targets but mostly because of its weapons. At least the objection of its conservative critics is to its methods rather than to its goals.
Probably not many Birchers would consciously embrace
the dogma of the Minutemen that "The time is past
when the American people might have saved themselves

[6] I emphasize the phrase "count themselves conservatives." Important
aspects of Mr. Goldwater's thought and policy are anything but conservative.

[7] See *The Radical Right*, p. 247.

by traditional political processes." [8] They are, however, urged to employ tactics which, by Welch's own admission are "mean and dirty" [9] and which have the effect, intended or no, of weakening those traditional political processes. The *John Birch Society Bulletin* states flatly that "for us to be *too civilized* is unquestionably to be defeated." [10] If defeat is based upon civility, the society would seem to be as safe as a snowball in the Arctic Circle. On at least one occasion, Birchites came to a meeting of the Young Republican Club of Los Angeles armed with revolvers —presumably to protect themselves against communist sympathizers inside the Grand Old Party! [11] Considering such methods, it should cause no surprise to discover that the John Birch Society bears a naked resemblance to some of the totalitarian groups it is aiming to eliminate. Furthermore it shares such groups' fear, distrust, and outright contempt for democracy. Mr. Welch promulgates the notion that "democracy" is "the worst of all forms of government. . . ." [12] Clearly his own organization is not in danger of dying from an overdose of it.

A group photograph of the Society's targets would make up a curious, conglomerate gathering of the prominent and the obscure. It would include, seated left to right,

[8] *On Target,* official journal of the Minutemen (November, 1964).

[9] *The Blue Book,* p. 74.

[10] Quoted in *The Radical Right,* pp. 248-49.

[11] Cf. "What's Wrong with the Far Right?" Distributed by Americans for Democratic Action, p. 6.

[12] *John Birch Society Bulletin* (July, 1964).

Kennedy, Nixon, Eisenhower, and Goldwater (now that
the latter is no longer useful to them) as well as a number
of lesser personages. Birchers got a great deal of notorious
mileage out of their founder's charges that Eisenhower
was a conscious, dedicated agent of the Communist
conspiracy. Birch defenders are quick to point out that
the charge was made by Welch before the Society was
founded. This is true. It is also true that Mr. Welch has
never repudiated it.

It is further true that the candy maker and his comrades
have an equally diverse group of organizations as targets:
The PTA ("Join your local PTA at the beginning of the
school year," the advice runs, "and go to work and capture
it." [18]), churches (note this, any who wonder what business
a churchman has discussing this topic), party structures,
school boards, library boards.

Bradley Morison, in a bit of verse entitled "Song of a
Modern Vigilante," has written:

> I sometimes fancy as I spy,
> That I excell the FBI
> Right now I'm making little lists
> Of folks I think are Communists
> I have no proof on anyone
> And yet the lists are lots of fun.
>
> All friends of foreign aid, I think
> Must be set down as rather pink

[18] *Ibid.* (September, 1960).

A little pinker, not far off,
I list perforce the college prof;
And pinker yet the student crowd
That lauds the Bill of Rights out loud.

U.N. supporters, as I've said,
Are always ipso facto red;
And redder still on my red lists
Are all the integrationists.
Just for good measure, in my labors
I add a few of my close neighbors.

Thus I rejoice that loyalty
Resides alone in you and me;
Although before my work is through
You may, good friend, be listed too.[14]

The first time I read that, I laughed. The *first* time.

I am not really afraid of the John Birch Society. Any organization that expects any large number of Americans seriously to credit the charge that General Eisenhower is traitorous will be tripped up by its own political delerium tremens. What I am afraid of is the John Birch mentality. Conscience is challenged and consequence is dark if we lightly acquiesce in that dissolution of the civil process where, as Judge Learned Hand has put it:

each man begins to eye his neighbor as a possible enemy, where nonconformity with the accepted creed, political as well as re-

[14] *The Catholic News* (February 24, 1962).

ligious, is a mark of disaffection; where denunciation, without specification or backing, takes the place of evidence; where orthodoxy chokes freedom of dissent; where faith in the eventual supremacy of reason has become so timid that we dare not enter our convictions in the open lists to win or lose.[15]

It is because the John Birch mentality threatens precisely this that the John Birch Society must be exposed and opposed.

II

A great deal of the remainder of the Radical Right, most of it—believe it or not—more radical and further right than the John Birch Society, is symbolized by the book *None Dare Call It Treason*. Were the issues not so grave, the charges not so serious, and the results not so fantastic, it would be tempting simply to dismiss the effort by saying, "None dares call it grammar!"[16] Unfortunately there is very much more to it than that.

No man, least of all myself, could hope to be an expert on all the subjects to which the author, one John A. Stormer, attempts to address himself. His fourteen chapters cover, in one sense or other, everything from education to economics treading over public communica-

[15] *The Spirit of Liberty, Papers of Learned Hand,* ed. Irving Dilliard (3rd rev. ed.; New York: Alfred A. Knopf, 1960), p. 284.

[16] In syntactical defense of Stormer it should be noted that he is quoting: "Treason doth never prosper, what's the reason?/For if it prosper, none dare call it treason" (Sir John Harrington).

tions, mental health, and organized labor on the way. I am not competent to judge thirteen of the fourteen chapters in the book. However, I can claim some small competence—perhaps almost as much as Mr. Stormer himself—in adjudging the adequacy and accuracy of his chapter on religion. On this basis there is large reason to hold that the tract should have been called *Some Dare Call It Slander.*

Let just one example suffice (and I could supply a dozen more[17]): Mr. Stormer quotes a Methodist publication as follows:

Jesus and Marx each lived in a time of social crisis . . . each believed that a new order lay within the reach of man . . . Both recognized . . . the need for social and moral reform . . . Both revealed a messianic sense of destiny . . . both men drew on their heritage of Old Testament prophecy to denounce evils in the world . . . Thus Marx and Christ were revolutionary leaders.[18]

However Stormer cynically hacks the facts from the case by amputating the quotation at its midsection. The remainder of what the author actually wrote was this:

[17] Cf. "A Report and Analysis of Chapter VII of *None Dare Call It Treason* by John A. Stormer," prepared by Henry M. Bullock, Editor, Methodist Church School Publications. This has been reprinted in *Christian Advocate* (October 22, 1964), p. 3.

[18] *None Dare Call It Treason* (Florissant, Mo.: Liberty Bell Press), pp. 129, 130.

Thus Marx and Christ were revolutionary leaders, *but their methods and goals lay far apart.* Jesus sought to change the minds and souls of man in a transformation or conversion (a "turning together") which would manifest itself in social justice and brotherhood. Marx, on the other hand, resolved to impose new political and economic patterns on society— molds into which men's minds would then be forced to fit.[19]

I find it impossible to believe that Stormer did not know what he was omitting. If one's anger sufficiently cools, he is obliged to remind Mr. Stormer that "a documented lie is still a lie,"[20] as a Methodist bishop was warning us a decade ago.

On the basis of such a sample—and, I repeat, it is merely a sample—it is not difficult to accept the judgment of the National Committee for Civic Responsibility that the entire book "is, at best, an incredibly poor job of research and documentation, and, at worst, a deliberate hoax and fraud." When the church is attacked in such a vicious and vitriolic fashion as this, continued silence is an affront to her faith and a denial of her Lord.

III

Space remains now only to make a few summary observations about the Radical Right as a whole as it collides—and collide it does—with the Christian creed.

[19] *Adult Student* (September, 1962), p. 21.
[20] G. Bromley Oxnam, *I Protest* (New York: Harper & Brothers, 1954), p. 92.

A montage of the frantic fringe's charges includes the allegation that most of our newspapers are spouting the communist line and the majority of our citizens duped by it; opposition to "ridiculous budgets" (I join them in that!) and to "unrestrained labor bossism" (I am against even *restrained* labor bossism); casting doubt on the loyalty of Billy Graham—as a radical, yet!—and labeling Mr. Goldwater as a "kosher conservative."[21] Again, these are but unsavory samples from the whole bitter brew.

It is time, then—far past time, really—that to these charges there be added, in Christian conscience, some countercharges.

Therefore I charge that the Radical Right is antimodern. Its leaders "are simply not able to consume without acute indigestion the acids of modernity."[22] What they are really protesting is not where our country is heading but where it no longer is, which is to say, in the eighteenth century. What they are objecting to is what America has become in the twentieth century. They could not even stumble into the twentieth century—unless they turned around.

I charge, secondly, that the Radical Right is a *pseudo*-conservative movement, a shoddy travesty of authentic conservatism and subversive of conservatism's abiding values.

[21] Statement from the National States Rights Party, quoted in "What Is Extremism?" p. 12.
[22] W. A. Kirk, "The Radical Right Dissected," *Concern* (December 1, 1964), p. 5.

I charge thirdly, that the Radical Right is soft on communism. At a time when domestic communism is frantically weak, international communism is aggressively strong. Yet the Right's obsession with the former threatens to immobilize our capacity to deal with the latter. Churchill reminds us that Mussolini raised himself to dictatorial power while promising to save Italy from communism. Those who have ears to hear, let them hear.

I charge, in the fourth place, that the Radical Right, like the Radical Left, is immorally committed to the doctrine that the ends justify the means. Means cannot be sundered from ends without doing violence to both.

I charge, finally, that the grounds for legitimate debate and the hopes of fruitful communication are being rashly cut away by the Radical Right's blind assumption that every opponent is an enemy and that every enemy must either be made to conform or caused to perish.

And I add to these charges the not very comforting, but very crucial, observation that radicalism, whether of the right or of the left, is one of the prices we pay for freedom.

Emerson once observed, "Conservatism makes no poetry, breathes no prayer, has no invention; it is all memory. Reform has no gratitude, no prudence, no husbandry . . . each is a good half but an impossible whole." The Radical Right is contemptuous of the part and destructive of the whole. Yet we need both the conservative with his memories and the liberal with his dreams. Each needs the other if either is to survive and if both are to flourish. As a Christian I am therefore conscience bound and honor pledged to protect the radical's right to exist—but to oppose what he stands for with all my heart and soul and mind and strength.

5

EXISTENTIALISM—PORCH OR DOMICILE?

Edmund Husserl once observed that in the life story of most important ideas three movements take place. In stage one the general reaction is: This is ridiculous. At stage two it is: Of course, everybody knows that. Then in the final movement an attempt is finally made seriously to ask: Just what does this mean? That sequence sounds something like this when translated into a specific proposal: (1) What! Voting rights for women! Absurd! (2) For generations our party has stood for universal suffrage. (3) Do you suppose we should include a woman on our national presidential ticket?

Such a dialectic marks the birth, growth, and maturation

of existentialism, or the philosophy of existence: (1) These men are mad. (2) Surely, were not Socrates and Isaiah saying the same thing? (3) What difference would it make if philosophers or housewives were existentialists? What is existentialism after all?

What follows is an attempted contribution to this third stage.

I

Some notes toward a definition of existentialism are in order.

Defining is made the more difficult because a great deal of stage two is still with us: "Everybody" is an existentialist, and "everybody" includes some intellectual elephants too numerous and too clumsy to get under one philosophical tent. It includes Sören Kierkegaard (1813-1835), a devout and iconoclastic Dane who, as the Spaniard Unamuno has written, "went to [his] final resting place after having stamped the truth in letters of fire across the cold dry forehead of his country's official church."[1] Under the same tent, on the other side, is the Frenchman Jean-Paul Sartre (a second cousin of Albert Schweitzer), who shares Kierkegaard's astringent honesty but who exercises it in the service of a thoughtful atheism. According to a popular magazine, Sartre has done more than any other man to shape contemporary thinking. That judgment is excessive,

[1] Miguel de Unamuno, *Perplexities and Paradoxes,* trans. Stuart Gross (New York: Philosophical Library, 1945), p. 51.

I would contend, but not worthless. But when the same verbal tent is used to try to cover both Kierkegaard and Sartre as well as everyone in between, definition is difficult. If everyone is an existentialist, no one is.

This observation suggests a second roadblock in the way of precise definition. In a sense "no one" is an existentialist. Most competent scholars would count among the philosophers of existence Karl Jaspers and Martin Heidegger; yet neither is particularly fond of the term *existentialist*. Why not? Recognizing that most sensitive people are not fond of labels, nevertheless, how does one define a term which its better proponents disavow?

Perhaps it is impossible. But some general characteristics can be stated, identifying if not uniting the movement as a whole, diverse as it is. The starting point for existentialism is the actual human situation rather than an abstraction, a concept, or an ideal. Secondly, all of these thinkers emphasize the uniqueness of the individual. They are primarily and in some cases obsessively concerned with the question: What does it mean to be a self? Consequently they hold that a man can come to terms with reality only by coming to terms with himself. And all existentialists, religious and atheistic alike, come down hard on the necessity of concern and commitment or at least engagement.

Trying to define existentialism is quite like attempting to define a scent: one may use real terms, but they belong to a world other than the world in which odors penetrate, nauseate, or please.[2] One may say "olfactory organs" or "emanations from a substance that affect the sense of smell," yet never smell a thing. Existentialism has been accused, unfairly in the large, of holding that definitions and intellectual precision are unimportant. Not so. Existentialism simply insists that one begins with the daffodil, not with the dictionary.

For this reason its best exponents have shown a refreshing preference for forms of indirect communication rather than for formal philosophy. Martin Buber, the Jew, was steeped in the parables of Hebrew folklore; Kierkegaard, the Christian, wrote extended narratives; Sartre, the atheist, prefers the drama and the short story.

For instance, when Kierkegaard wanted to give form and color to the fact of human guilt, he did so parabolically:

The case of the guilty man who journeys through life to eternity is like that of the murderer who with the speed of the railway train fled from the place where he perpetuated his crime. Alas, just under the railway coach where he sat ran the electric telegraph with its signal and the order for his apprehension at the next station. When he reached the station and alighted

[2] Cf. Carl Michalson, *Christianity and the Existentialists* (New York: Charles Scribner's Sons, 1956), p. 3.

It may be objected that this is a problem implicit in all definitions. That is so, but the difficulty seems to me particularly intense in a philosophy like existentialism. The familiar triad of Hegelianism can almost be expressed algebraically. Thesis, antithesis, and synthesis are intellectual terms. Anguish, despair, and freedom are not.

from the coach he was arrested. In a way he brought the denunciation with him.[3]

For instance, when Sartre wants to give shape and darkness to the fact of death, he does so by writing a penetrating short story, "The Wall." When I read it, I am not simply examining an absorbing and ironic account of a young man facing death; I find myself pondering —painfully or faithfully—my death.

When one ponders these parables, follows these narratives, experiences these dramas, and when one seeks from them a definition of existentialism, one undergoes a curious response. It is very like stepping barefoot on a thistle —suddenly one is much more aware of himself than of the thistle.

II

Let us reflect now, in a little more detail, upon the major themes of the philosophy of existence.

One of them is illustrated by Kierkegaard in these whimsical, deeply serious words:

What the philosophers say about reality is often just as disappointing as it is when you read a sign at a second-hand store: "Ironing done here." If you should come with your clothes to get them ironed, you'd be fooled, for only the sign is for sale.[4]

[3] *The Sickness Unto Death,* trans. Walter Lowrie (Anchor ed.; New York: Doubleday & Company, 1954), p. 255.

[4] Quoted in Marjorie Grene, *Introduction to Existentialism* (Chicago: University of Chicago Press, 1959), p. 35.

This is the daffodil and dictionary problem all over again. The Russian novelist Dostoevsky puts it somewhat more formally when he has one of his characters say that "reason is nothing but reason . . . while will is a manifestation of the whole life . . . including reason . . . And although our life, in this manifestation of it, is often worthless, yet it is life and not simply extracting square roots." Then the character adds, of reason, "some things, perhaps, it will never learn." [5] Philosophers have a technical and not completely apt phrase for this theme of the philosophy of existence: *Existence precedes essence.* Perhaps it can be more simply stated by the aphorism, *Thinking does not make it so.* We reminded the humanist, in chapter two, that the important thing about science is the scientist. Now in a little different sense we are reminded by the existentialist that philosophically the most important thing about philosophy is the philosopher. Existentialism is a revolt against the role of the philosopher as observer and for the role of the philosopher as participant.

A second major motif of the philosophy of existence is the importance yet the isolation of the individual.[6] Sartre has published a short story entitled "Intimacy." The title is very misleading. The story portrays very little of any intimacy. It describes bodily contact, not intimacy. Distance is its watchword, and detachment is its theme. Sartre is

[5] *The Short Novels of Dostoevsky,* trans. Constance Garnett, "Notes from Underground" (New York: The Dial Press, 1945), p. 147.

[6] A major exception here is Karl Jaspers.

here typical of the existential conviction that genuine contact (real intimacy) with other people inevitably issues in conflict. As he puts it in his memorable production *No Exit*: "Hell is—other people!" Therefore those other people are not to be permitted to impinge upon or to interfere with *me*.

The third basic theme of the philosophy of existence, arising out of the second, is that freedom is fundamental. As the Dostoevsky character earlier quoted phrases it, "I may degrade and defile myself, but I am not anyone's slave." [7] He is not a slave of anyone else, we might add by way of anticipated comment; he *is* the slave of himself.

Since freedom is fundamental, being decisive and making decisions are crucial. The word *crucial* is used here in a doubly etymological sense: decisiveness is the crux, and decisions may crucify you. To choose a mate or a major is probably to limit and anyway to change all your subsequent choices. Thus Martin Buber comments, "If there were a devil, it would not be one who decided against God, but one who, in eternity, came to no decision." [8]

These, then, are three major themes of most philosophies of existence. Several comments are in order.

Comments in Defense

Sartre's almost blatant atheism and his quite militant doctrine of freedom are his ways of rejecting any world-

[7] *The Short Novels of Dostoevsky*, p. 194.
[8] *I and Thou* (New York: Charles Scribner's Sons, 1958), p. 52.

view that would determine or predetermine man. He assumes that if God were real, this would mean that man's good would be decided in advance no matter what he chose to do or neglected to do with his freedom. I think that Kierkegaard, whose belief in God was almost as blatant as is Sartre's unbelief, would agree with Sartre here *if* affirming God meant denying human freedom. If belief in God were to mean what Sartre takes it to mean, most of us would have to join him, reluctantly but consistently, in his atheism. Hence the Christian will probably judge that such existentialists are right in what they affirm about freedom but wrong in what they deny about God.

Secondly, the familiar charge that to be atheistic is to be chaotic in one's ethics is not necessarily true and is not meant to be true. The Frenchwoman Simone de Beauvoir writes that

far from God's absence authorizing all license, the contrary is the case. . . . because his acts are definitive, absolute engagements. He bears the responsibility for a world which is not the work of a strange power, but of himself.[9]

What Sartre, for instance, is fighting for and writing for

[9] *The Ethics of Ambiguity,* trans. Bernard Frechtman (New York: Philosophical Library, 1948), pp. 15-16. "For clearly," as Kenneth Hamilton has written, "only religious fanaticism would maintain that an atheist is *ipso facto* an immoral person, and yet there is nothing fanatical about the belief that moral standards are vulnerable unless they are supported by religious faith." From "Life in the House that *Angst* Built," *The Hibbert Journal,* LVII (October, 1958), 51.

is not a licentious ethic but an autonomous one. What we must remember in evaluating this is that Sartre spent his earlier years as a member of the French resistance during the Second World War, fighting against the sick autonomy of an antisocial society, namely Nazi Germany. Existentialists, like others, sometimes live worse than they write (sometimes they live better). They do not aim, however, to destroy ethics but to provide an ethic for situations in which they can see no guidelines.[10] What *do* you do when your country is governed by a mad ruler, or when your race is legally bound by immoral laws? It is to such questions that the existentialist "ethics of ambiguity" addresses itself.

Thirdly, the existential emphasis upon the importance and inevitability of decision sometimes leads to the erroneous conclusion that decisiveness is good for its own sake. Without approving immobilizing indecision or lukewarm concern, we would have to insist that *what* one decides is of a piece with the decision itself. The decision *whether* to marry cannot be legitimately made (one can even say, cannot be morally made) apart from the decision about *whom* to marry. For the purposes of thinking about them they may be separated, but they belong and are important only together.

Again, the existentialist in his emphasis upon the "autonomous" individual at least sees the problem. Sartre writes,

[10] It does seem to me, however, that Sartre is a bit more vulnerable here than is, for instance, De Beauvoir.

probably more profoundly than he knows, that "man is the being whose project is to be God." [11] One cannot escape the observation that if Sartre had followed up on this insight, if he had seen what he calls man's project as instead man's problem, he would have made more progress. It might have landed him far up on the frontiers of the book of Genesis!

Furthermore, to assert the fundamental isolation of the individual is to blink at one of the most important insights of both psychology and theology. Decades ago George Herbert Mead taught us that the self becomes a self only in a community of other selves; the child, for instance, is probably not aware of himself until he becomes aware of others. What social psychology suggests, biblical psychology confirms: "The body is one and has many members, and all . . . are one body" (I Cor. 12:12). There are times in which it almost seems that Sartre sees how untenable is his view of the self. He writes, for example, "I am not the foundation of my own being." [12] Yet he consistently fails to pursue the implications of this insight, which is too bad, for it would have led him precisely to those "other people" who, because he is isolated from them, he thinks are hell.

Once more, we are obligated to agree, however reluctantly, with the existentialist that estrangement *is* every-

[11] *Existentialism and Human Emotions* (New York: Philosophical Library, 1957), p. 63.
[12] *Ibid.*, p. 57.

where. Brother is divided from brother, son from mother, race from race, nation from nation, man from God. If philosophies purporting to offer a world-view were more consistent in keeping this estranged world in view, as the existentialists have, then the real situation in which we live and love, and hate and die would be more helpfully addressed and more healthfully healed.

Moreover, the answer to this estrangement, if we have learned our existential lessons well, lies in the quality of our relationships rather than just in the subtlety of our arguments. The church, of course, would not have had to relearn this lesson from such a seemingly alien source had she kept close to some of her own very existential documents, one of which affirms, "If one member suffers, all suffer together; if one member is honored, all rejoice together" (I Cor. 12:26).

Critical Comments

Existentialists have at least seen with painful clarity the brokenness of human life, a brokenness in which we all participate and to which we all contribute. Existentialists have at least stated that felt-in-the-bones brokenness. They have steadfastly—one could almost say faithfully—refused to coat it with the soothing frauds of the everyday. Some of them may have engaged in too much of what Karl Barth has referrred to as "existential screaming." Nevertheless we should ponder the significance of Paul Tillich's statement that "one does not feel spiritually threatened by something which is not an element of oneself"[13] before we stop our ears to the scream. For surely this curious, contradictory, live, and elusive philosophy has sensed deeply some values which escape language and defy analysis.

Kierkegaard predicted, with uncanny prescience and (one guesses) not a little amusement, that one day men would take his insights and set them into a system, freeze them into a philosophy, the very thing he was protesting against. If he was right in his protest—and I believe he was—then the answer to our chapter title question—porch or domicile—for Christians at least, is *porch*. As Carl Michalson observed:

Existentialism is an approach to a house. The Christian does not live on the porch and the existentialist does not enter the house without ceasing to be an existentialist. There seems to be a widespread conviction in theology today that the title "existential theology" is a tautology. I would call it a contradiction. Existentialism is the expression of the fundamental meaninglessness of existence. The Christian faith is just the opposite: the revelation of fundamental meaning.[14]

Existentialism as a mode of philosophizing has much to teach us. Existentialism as a philosophy has much to unlearn.

[13] *The Courage to Be* (New Haven: Yale University Press, 1952), p. 141.
[14] *The Rationality of Faith* (New York: Charles Scribner's Sons, 1963), p. 18.

Kierkegaard once wrote, in words as beautiful as they are true, that

A poet is an unhappy being whose heart is torn by secret sufferings, but whose lips are so strangely formed that when the sighs and cries escape them, they sound like beautiful music. His fate is like that of the unfortunate victims whom the tyrant Phalaris imprisoned in a brazen bull, and slowly tortured over a steady fire; their cries could not reach the tyrant's ears so as to strike terror into his heart: when they reached his ears they sounded like sweet music. And men crowd about the poet and say to him: "You must sing for us again soon." Which is as much as to say, "May fresh sufferings torture your soul, but may your lips be formed as before; for the cries would only frighten us, but the music is delicious." [15]

That could have been written by Jeremiah. Or by Jesus. I am confident that both would have been receptive to it.

[15] "Diapsalmata" in *Either/Or*, trans. W. Lowrie *et al.* (2 vols.; Princeton: Princeton University Press, 1944), I, 15.

6

THE COST OF SUBSCRIBING TO PLAYBOY *

If the young church secretary had known whose card she was placing in the file, probably her hand would have quivered, her voice deepened, her pulse quickened, her spine tingled, and her composure disappeared. The card tells us that the registrant was born on April 9, 1926, that he was presently a senior at the university, that his home was Chicago, and that he preferred Methodism (or at least could spell it). His name: Hugh Marston Hefner.

Nothing on the card indicates any sustained relationship

* I owe this title, and permission to use it, to Chaplain Lawrence Meredith of the College of the Pacific.

between that student and the campus church. I am sorry about that, for *Playboy* could be an even better magazine if Mr. Hefner had bothered to subject the religion he brought down from Chicago to a little empirical analysis. Since he seemingly did not, the brand of religion he subjects to almost monthly editorial excoriation is a nearly comical blend of childhood memory, Hefnerian hallucination, and rural residue.

I am sorry about that for another reason. Mr. Hefner seems to be a gracious, charming, fascinating, upbeat character whom it would be fun to get to know.

Anyway the student graduated and returned to his urban hutch in Chicago. (Incidentally, considering the near-obsession he has about Puritanism, there is surely some just irony in the fact that his street address during those days was New England Avenue.) After working for *Esquire* for a short period, he resigned, scraped together six hundred dollars, borrowed another six thousand, and parlayed the sum into one of the most startling and precocious financial empires in the history of journalism.

Playboy magazine today has a readership greater than the subscription lists of all of the scholarly journals combined. Written and edited especially for the younger male (more than half of its readers are under the age of thirty), its appeal is slanted toward the urbanized, educated, sophisticated, detached and unattached member of what Hefner calls the "upbeat generation."

He partly explains what he means by the upbeat generation by contrasting it with the "beat generation." The latter,
he points out, was a colorful but negative turning of the
back upon the conforming and security-conscious society
of its elders. The upbeats, says Hefner, are more numerous
than the beats; they buy more razor blades and take
more baths. Nevertheless the beats and the upbeats share
a rebellious spirit and a readiness to cast off the chains of
sameness and security.

It would, however, be a mistake to think *Playboy*'s
sizeable and growing cult is just so many beardless beats
who bathe. Hence in an early issue of the magazine, what
was meant by a playboy was explained:

He isn't a wastrel or a ne'er-do-well; he might be a successful
business executive, a man in the arts, a college professor, an
architect or an engineer. What sets him apart is his *point of
view.* . . . [He] must find pleasure in his work, without re-
garding it as the end and all of living; . . . a man sensitive to
pleasure, who—without acquiring the stigma of the voluptuary
or the dilettante—can live life to the hilt.[1]

I take the editor to be honest in that judgment. What
seems to have escaped his perception is the total effect of his
magazine as distinct from the editorial intent. Its overall
effect is precisely an appeal to and an encouragement of

[1] As summarized in "The Playboy Philosophy," Installment 19, *Playboy*
(December, 1964).

the kind of person he says the playboy is not, namely, the dilettante. This appeal goes under a very ancient name: hedonism.[2] The term comes from a Greek word meaning sweet or pleasant and hence has come to be known as the philosophy of pleasure. In its probably earliest articulation it was stated by Aristippus and the Cyreniacs in the fourth and third centuries B.C. In modern times it was prolated in a more sophisticated form by Jeremy Bentham (1748-1832). In between and since it has had a host of practitioners and spokesmen. *Playboy* magazine may be a new journalistic venture, although a little knowledge of, say, French literature makes even that claim a little dubious. However that may be, the philosophy on which it is based is almost literally as old as hell. The announcement that man can be sensuous and selfish can hardly be called intellectually startling, whatever one's efforts to give it intellectual respectability.

Those efforts in the present case are a considerable if inconspicuous feature of nearly every month's issue. They are called by the editor, with great seriousness and not a little presumption, "The Playboy Philosophy." True, Hefner admits that he is no philosopher, an announcement which scarcely overwhelms one with surprise.[3]

Nor, for that matter, is "The Playboy Philosophy" a

[2] Cf. Joseph Fletcher, *Situation Ethics* (Philadelphia: The Westminster Press, 1966), p. 47.

[3] His intellectual indebtedness to John Stuart Mill, and particularly to Mill's essay *On Liberty*, is pronounced. Note also the comments of Joseph Fletcher in *Situation Ethics*, p. 47.

philosophy, if one understands that the word still means to careful users of the language, "the love of wisdom." Hefner does write a great deal about the wisdom of love, but that is another matter with which we shall deal in due course.

In fact, the editor writes a great deal. The result is usually clear if not very exciting prose. Some months (when, I suppose, he is harried by the hutchness of life) he relies upon quoting from old term papers and articles written while in college or from edited transcripts of long radio interview-discussions. He has at his disposal what must be an almost insomniac research staff, and thus his editorials bounce with facts and, of course, figures. Thus far his editorial efforts total more than 250,000 words, which is about 30,000 words more than Plato used in his five great *Dialogues*. Here endeth the similarity.

In spite of the jocular tone with which I have dealt with Hefner's philosophical and literary pretensions, he is clearly an editorial genius and an image-maker par excellence. We shall do our culture and ourselves a great disservice by default if we do not take the *effect* of his efforts with great seriousness. Indeed, anyone who thinks Hefner is not being taken that way anyway simply does not know his newsstands or his bull sessions.

The editor has a great many opinions, some of them well substantiated, most of them well documented, on a great many subjects. In a survey volume such as this,

obviously, only the tersest of summaries is permissible.
Nevertheless let us try.

I

One reads with interest and approval that our national
concerns can no longer be defined by our national borders;
that totalitarian methods are out of bounds to democratic
procedure, even when aimed at combating totalitarianism,
whether of the right or of the left. Most lawyers will
agree with his summary (not quite in a nutshell, but in
a coconut shell perhaps) of our sex laws as a hopelessly
contradictory hodgepodge of hypocritical chaos. Many of us
will concur in his commendation of the revised Illinois
Criminal Code which removes the pall of illegality from
the sex act—any isolated sex act—between consenting
adults, so long as it is performed in private. (By the way,
it is curious to notice how the people who say one cannot
legislate morality react to that! However, the question
with which the Criminal Code is dealing is not, appropriately, one of morality but of legality.[4]) Many also think
that his analysis of censorship and his efforts to minimize
it make more sense than do the combined moralizings of
many churchmen.

[4] Such codal revisions do not, as is so often charged, "condone" or "ap-
prove" immorality. They simply constitute legislative recognition that
"immoral" and "illegal" are not necessarily interchangeable terms and
that sanctions concerning the former are properly the domain of the
home, the church, and the school. Cf. *Smith-Hurd Illinois Annotated
Statutes* (Chicago: Burdette Smith Company, 1964), chapter 38, "Criminal
Law and Procedure," especially pp. xiii ff and 557 ff.

I should genuinely like to know more about Mr. Hefner's childhood religion. His antipathy for Roman Catholicism is stark. The frequency with which his employment of the words "religion" or "Protestant" is accompanied by the epithetical use of words like "puritanical," "legalistic," "moralistic," "fundamentalist," and "antisexual" makes it clear that he does not possess even the foggiest notion of what has been happening in the leading theological seminaries for almost as many years as Hefner is old. Some evidence, however, suggests that he may be shifting toward a bit more open stance here, as a result of the fact that some churchmen are honestly endeavoring to take his editorial efforts seriously.[5] His understanding, or misunderstanding, of the separation of church and state most often comes down to the separation of religion and life. He protests that he is no theologian—again, a superfluous admission—but he theologizes all over the place.

It is in his view of sex that he is so nearly right yet so

[5] Cf. the edited transcript of the four-session radio conversation with three New York clergymen, which transcript makes up the major portion of installments 19, 20, 21, and 22 of "The Playboy Philosophy." Cf. especially Hefner's closing statement in the first of these four, *Playboy* (December, 1964).

Dean Theodore Peterson of the University of Illinois' College of Journalism and Communications is a nationally renowned authority on magazine journalism. He has stated that "whatever their reaction, the clergy and the religious press seem to have treated Hefner more kindly and more seriously than some of the secular media." Professor Peterson further characterized one of *Life* magazine's treatments of Hefner as marked "with a prurience it would have found offensive in *Playboy.*" *Columbia Journalism Review,* V (Spring, 1966), 35.

perilously wrong. I should say that he is right on so many
matters that it is difficult for the average person (the
average college student, for instance) to detect where he is
wrong.

I am personally grateful to Mr. Hefner for the chuckle
he has put back into the subject of sex. I am personally
unsympathetic with those who have lost their sense of
sexual humor, whether those who, on the one hand, leer
at it, or those who, on the other, are so stiff-necked and
insecure in their cold morality that they give the impression
that they were starched before they were washed.

Furthermore I hold that Hefner rightly indicts the
Judeo-Christian tradition for antisexual attitudes. To indict,
remember, is to accuse of a crime. It *is* nothing short of
criminal that religious people should have forgotten *the
biblical and insightful understanding that sex is good in
the sight of God*. What Hefner does not understand is
that *antisexuality is a crime—or more accurately, a heresy
—from the Judeo-Christian point of view too*. But if anything he is too gentle with the church here, not too harsh.

Hefner is right that Western religion has almost completely ignored the sexual needs of the single adult. Hefner
is right when he says we have paid too little attention to
that explosive gap between the young adolescent's physical
maturity and his much later social and educational readiness for marriage. Hefner is right that many, many
marriages take place too soon between people who are
trying to establish contact with another person mostly

because they have never made contact in the first place with themselves. And Hefner is surely right that, as a result of such humorless, negative, and ignorant attitudes, many people are "lost in the gap between complete permissiveness and the traditional . . . morality of old." [6] If churchmen would take the trouble to read what Hefner is writing instead of assuming that the magazine has only one page in it, and that one naughty, they would discover, in many instances, that he simply is not saying what they accuse him of saying and that, on many issues, they have an ally not a foe.

II

Wherein, then, is he wrong? What *is* the cost of subscribing to *Playboy?* I would list five costs.

The first is *a cost in realism.* Consider the following advertisement, appearing in this magazine which prides itself in realism:

Dynamic Discovery! *New Male Scrubbed Jeans . . . soft as a kiss!* . . . smooth as a shoulder . . . soft to the touch . . . loaded with instant comfort [I had thought, strange me that I am, that what they were filled with was hairy legs], thanks to an exclusive *Male Process! . . . you're more of a man in MALE.*[7]

Anson Mount, editor of "The Playboy Forum," upon

[6] "The Playboy Philosophy," Installment 21, *Playboy* (February, 1965).
[7] *Playboy* (October, 1965), p. 193.

reading an earlier draft of this chapter, phoned to remind
me that the magazine is not responsible for writing its
advertisements—only for accepting or rejecting them. That
is of course true. It is also true that this advertisement—
and hundreds like it—was accepted and that the total
effect of the magazine contributes to an image of reality
which is most unreal. I have no wish to engage in
journalistic proof-texting. One could dispute one part of
the magazine by quoting another part over against it.
Perhaps not many young men "buy" the world of expensive stereos, fast Jaguars, and faster women which
Playboy offers as real. So far as some do, however, they
are purchasing a slick and misleading counterfeit.

The unrealism of *Playboy* may be further seen in the
fact that most women simply do not look like the bovine
bunnies the magazine portrays.[8] Any young man who
thinks they do is in for a big surprise some day, provided
the playboy can still be surprised by anything. Mort Sahl
overstated it only slightly when he humorously accused
Hefner of bringing on an entire generation of young men
conditioned to believe that the typical girl folds in three
places and has a staple in her navel. That is realism?

Moreover the second cost, a consequence of the first, is

[8] Cf. "Hugh Hefner: That Dear, Dangerous Old-Fashioned Boy,"
Joanne Pettet, *Cosmopolitan* (May, 1966), pp. 82-83. This article is a
précis of criticism of some of Hefner's arguments from the point of view
of a sophisticated woman.

a cost in aesthetics. The magazine's women lose the beauty contest *when judged by Hefner's own standards.* He contends that the female form is beautiful. Big news! He further contends that there is nothing intrinsically wrong with contemplating that form. I agree. However, I invite you to compare these women who voluptuate all over his pages with the stunning and authentically feminine beauties who appear as models in many of the advertisements accepted by *The New Yorker.* A famous manufacturer was in this business long before Hefner, except that he had the honesty to call his cover girl by her right name: Elsie the Cow.

The third (and this is a *cost* women pay for subscribing to *Playboy*) is one of *dispensability.* One of the important, if not much emphasized, parts of the *Playboy* philosophy about women is what may be called the doctrine of use. Women may be used like an attractive, if expensive, accessory and then, like any other accessory, replaced next year when fashions change. I suppose we cannot argue with Hefner's contention that a woman has a right to place herself on a par with a scented handkerchief or an alligator belt or a sniff of Klompen Kloggen tobacco. But how any even moderately intelligent woman could fall for such a line is several billion light years beyond my understanding.

From any reasonably enlightened ethical point of view —to say nothing of Christian doctrine—there is no more

grave abuse of any personality than to use a person as if
he or she were a mere thing. A person is a being, important,
valued, and cherished in his own right and for his own
sake. Consequently it is plainly wrong to treat him as a
mere instrument of your own pleasure, reliever of your
own frustrations, or object of your own domination. (By
the way, this is true whether such exploitation takes place
within or outside the marriage bond.) One can anticipate
Mr. Hefner's protest here that he is talking about "consenting adults." To this we must reply that if a woman
consents to being kicked in the stomach, she has still been
kicked, as any gentleman knows.

The fourth cost of *Playboy*'s philosophy of sex is,
oddly enough, *a cost in sex itself*. The most damaging
charge against the magazine is not that the publication is
immoral. It assuredly is not; the magazine's antimoralizing
is one of the places it is right. Rather the most crumbling
charge against the magazine is that it is antisexual. I
firmly believe that its *playboys are afraid of the mystery
and the grandeur of sex*. They know no other way to
deal with their fears than to take this great and awful
gift from God and trivialize it. They spend so much time
and expend so much energy wrapping—or unwrapping
—the package and curling the ribbon that they totally
miss the fact that someone slipped them an empty carton.
Mr. Hefner is forever pulling the pigtails of Puritanism.
Any fifth-grade teacher could tell him why.

A final *cost* is one *in relationships*. Katherine Anne Porter describes this cost in a profoundly revealing passage in her novel *Ship of Fools*. A girl's reflection upon her experience with what is called free love:

They had agreed in the beginning not to marry because they must be free, marriage was a bond cramping and humiliating to civilized beings: yet what was this tie between them but marriage, and marriage of the worst sort, with all the restraints and jealousies and burdens, but with none of its dignity, none of its warmth and protection, no honest acknowledgment of faith and intention.[9]

This relational cost of subscribing to the *Playboy* philosophy implies quite clearly that a man simply cannot treat his relationship to a woman like a beach towel to be put on or laid aside according to the rainclouds or sunshine of his whims. As Harvey Cox has written, "anyone with a modicum of experience with a woman knows it can't be done." [10] A temporary relationship with a woman is not a *relation*ship at all. It is a tragicomedy—without meaning, without character, without dignity, and without climax.

The harsh fact is that the playboy is so wordly wise that he is stupid. For all his experiences, he has never really known a woman—which is, I am sure, the costliest cost of all.

[9] (Boston: Little, Brown and Company, 1962), p. 145.
[10] *The Secular City*, p. 203.

Any Christian critique of playboyism must hold that the magazine and the philosophy it propounds, far from taking sex seriously, is simplistically casual about it—a fact, by the way, which the editor himself acknowledges.[11]

If one wants a philosophy that does take man's sexuality with profound seriousness, I suggest one propounded by a very alive young man whose name was Jesus of Nazareth. In contrast to the playboy, who arrogantly assumes that others are for his use, Jesus has been appropriately called, the man for others.[12] It was he who said, citing the tradition out of which he came,

. . . he who made them from the beginning made them male and female . . . "For this reason a man shall leave his father and mother and be joined to his wife, and the two shall become one." . . . So they are no longer two but one. What therefore God has joined together, let not man put asunder (Matt. 19:4-6).

The reference is to one total and indissoluble unity so completely permanent and so permanently complete that neither person is ever again the same.

I would contend, in short, that Jesus takes man's sexuality —and the dynamics of the personal relationships it involves

[11] "The Playboy Philosophy," Installment 19, *Playboy* (December, 1964).

[12] Cf. Dietrich Bonhoeffer, *Prisoner for God,* ed. Eberhard Bethge, trans. Reginald H. Fuller (New York: The Macmillan Company, 1954), p. 179; also John A. T. Robinson, *Honest to God* (Philadelphia: The Westminster Press, 1963), pp. 64-83.

and requires—more seriously than Hefner ever has, or could.

His is a costly philosophy too, one embodying both the love of wisdom and the wisdom of love. But it is worth the price.

AFTERWORD

1

The root sin of each of these creeds is idolatry.

Idolatry is, in contemporary theology, a fairly sophisticated notion. It has to be if the commandment against the making of graven images is to have any residual meaning today. Few men are tempted to treat a crudely carved fetish or even an elaborately engraved chalice as if it in itself were important—probably none of the readers of this volume is tempted. There are, however, other ways to act as if God were not God. A number of these ways are secreted or set forth in the creeds we have been surveying in the foregoing chapters. All images are not graven.

Secularism, as we have seen, is a latent and practical atheism, as distinguished from an overt and a theoretical one. Its adherents belong to a variety of religious communions or to none. What marks the lot is that they *act* as if their own devisings—intellectual, economic, even religious—were God.

Humanism, except that high humanism which arises out of the Judeo-Christian tradition and which characterizes that tradition at its best, idolatrously substitutes the lesser for the whole. It understands, often insightfully, that man is a being of frightful and magnificent powers. It does not understand—or, in some cases will not—that these powers are not self-explanatory. In the name of taking man seriously it leaves him seriously fragmented, then worships the fragment. Fragmented worship, as well as false worship, is idolatry.

On the other hand, the Christian creed is authentically humanistic because it is not exclusively so. It is profoundly appreciative of the humanist's high estimate of man, at the same time insisting that man does not, dares not, and cannot feed upon his own fingers. Self-worship is still idolatry.

Marxism's idol is a peculiar, if not terribly original, interpretation of history, but one it pursues with a passion and a singularity which can legitimately and safely be given only to the God of the history being interpreted. It

is thus so nearly right yet so perilously wrong and, in
some of its manifestations, demonic. Most of what is
even theoretically defensible about Marxism is rooted in
the religion it either loudly denies or cynically tolerates.
Marxism is religion gone sour, idolatrously.

The philosophy of the Radical Right is the most dis-
parate of any of the creeds under consideration. Strictly
speaking it is not a philosophy, but a rallying point for a
socio-economic fundamentalism about history, especially
about national history. Its devotees include representatives
of that "successful" but insecure class whose ideological
ancestors in the nineteenth century were Know Nothings
and in the eighteenth century were Tories. It has also
proved itself distressingly attractive to a monochromatic
(mostly white) collection of bigots. Very few authentic
conservatives feather the right wing.

Its membership makeup is not, however, our present
point. The issue is its idolatry. As we saw in chapter
four, its God is its image of what the nation once was,
or what it imagines the nation was. The clearest practical
example of this may be noted among its pious or churchly
constituency. If the social pronouncements or the social
action of their church differs from their rightist God, it is
automatically assumed that it is the church which has
fallen into heresy. Stated bluntly this means that, if the
rightist churchman is forced to choose between his political predilections and his religious requirements, the latter

always loses. The radical rightist is a political man first and a religious man second, and he is the latter only if the former permits.[1] He is thus guilty of idolatry.

The idolatry of existentialism is a little more difficult to identify, in part because, as we saw in chapter five, few are willing to claim the name and because the existentialist's spectrum stretches from the atheistic to the devout. I should want to acknowledge here that many of the latter have made a profound and, in many ways, pivotal contribution to the understanding of the Christian creed itself. The former, however, have schematized and elevated one or another element (freedom, despair, being) to the status of God himself. Therefore they have broken the first and second commandments.

It should have been evident to the reader that, in chapter six, we were using the "playboy" as an inclusive symbol, subsuming under that heading many whose philosophical commitment, consciously or unconsciously, is hedonism. The public can hardly be blamed for the popular, if not entirely accurate, identification of this commitment with sex. This equation is unfortunate, for (among other reasons) it isolates a mere, although serious, symptom of something much deeper—namely, the self centered upon itself. Psychologically this is called egotism; theologically it is called sin; biblically it is called idolatry.

---

[1] This is not, of course, a phenomenon unique among rightists, but it is decidedly pronounced among them.

Idolatry, then, is the root sin of each of these creeds
with which Christianity collides.

II

It would be repetitious, even in an Afterword, to set
down the distinctive tenets of these idolatries. The primer
of their belief was sketched in each chapter. It is necessary,
however, to face some issues raised by the very use of the
word "creed" in their connection.[2]

As I implied in the Preface, a real creed corresponds to
the three parts of a work of art: (1) the apprehension of
an experience on the part of the artist, (2) the expression
of it, (3) the action of response on the part of others.
These three elements hold even if the creed is not a
religious one. On this basis, all six of the creeds surveyed
qualify as real.

Secondly, these six, like the creeds of the church, are
intended to exclude what they understand as error almost
as much as they are designed to express what they affirm
as truth.

Again, all six (in varying degrees) emphasize action,
the crucial answer to the question any creed should raise:
"So what! What should I do about it?" Christianity has
reason to be humble in the presence of these adversaries.
Christianity has too often and too easily tolerated the

[2] On the nature of the creed for the religious community of faith,
see the author's *Portrait of the Church: Warts and All* (Nashville: Abingdon Press, 1964), pp. 58 and 66-67.

damning and damaging burden of deedless creeds. So far as the collisions recounted herein remind her of her apostasy at the point of action, she should be uneasily grateful.

What one cannot do with these creeds, however, is to sing them, as Calvin insisted we should. "Glory to man in the highest" and "praised be our Father, dialectical materialism" are neither tempting nor likely antiphons.

Yet creed is essentially song. A creed more resembles a poem than it does a syllogism. A creed is only the indirect object of faith—a groping, lilting, struggling, singing result of an encounter with the real—for the religious man, an encounter with God. When you start weighing each word in a love letter (saying, I wonder what he meant by that? Are my eyes really like a summer pool in a cornflower gown?), you are no longer in love. A creed which begins as dogma dies as a dirge. A creed which begins as love song lives as a faith.

We must insist, then, against this volume's title, that there is a sense in which these six are *not* creeds: they cannot be sung.

Some readers may ask, with some justice, why atheism itself was not included in our survey. The reason is practical and empirical. If my observation and experience are at all accurate, theoretical or abstract atheism is neither a live option nor a serious threat in our time. It is extremely dubious whether Robert Ingersoll would be listened to today if he were able to recommence his attempted demolition of divinity.

Still other readers may ask why the author has not stated more explicitly and at some length the content of the Christian creed over against these other creeds. What is meant by Christian humanism? How does Christianity take sex more seriously than *Playboy* does? These questions too have some point. Quite inevitably I have been operating from and writing out of some theological presuppositions. I can only state that the questions imply another book, which may some day be written, and that the decision to do it this way, while arbitrary, was taken upon the advice of several of the early readers of the typed script.

W. H. Auden is, in my opinion, one of the best poets writing in English today. In a note to one of his prose poems he makes a statement which sounds as if he is the biggest dogmatist too. He writes, "I can only hope that this piece will seem meaningless to those who are not professing Christians." [3]

There is a sense in which no creed can be understood except from the inside. To that extent my efforts to be fair in these analyses have been unavailing. Yet even though, as a Christian, I am outside what I have endeavored to describe, I have tried at least to be *empathetically* outside.

[3] Note to "Depravity: a Sermon" in *The Collected Poetry of W. H. Auden* (New York: Random House, 1945), p. 242.

If I have succeeded in that and if, in addition, I have added some accuracy to my empathy and a little insight to my critique, then perhaps the reader will think the result worthwhile. It is with that purpose and with this hope that this little volume is sent forth.

Index